Mexican Air Fryer Cookbook 2021

1000-Day Authentic Mexican Recipes to Fry, Bake, Grill, and Roast with Your Air Fryer

Smurs Jobls

© Copyright 2021 Smurs Jobls - All Rights Reserved.

In no way is it legal to reproduce, duplicate, or transmit any part of this document by either electronic means or in printed format. Recording of this publication is strictly prohibited, and any storage of this material is not allowed unless with written permission from the publisher. All rights reserved.

The information provided herein is stated to be truthful and consistent, in that any liability, regarding inattention or otherwise, by any usage or abuse of any policies, processes, or directions contained within is the solitary and complete responsibility of the recipient reader. Under no circumstances will any legal liability or blame be held against the publisher for any reparation, damages, or monetary loss due to the information herein, either directly or indirectly.

Respective authors own all copyrights not held by the publisher.

Legal Notice:

This book is copyright protected. This is only for personal use. You cannot amend, distribute, sell, use, quote or paraphrase any part of the content within this book without the consent of the author or copyright owner. Legal action will be pursued if this is breached.

Disclaimer Notice:

Please note the information contained within this document is for educational and entertainment purposes only. Every attempt has been made to provide accurate, up-to-date and reliable, complete information. No warranties of any kind are expressed or implied. Readers acknowledge that the author is not engaging in the rendering of legal, financial, medical or professional advice.

By reading this document, the reader agrees that under no circumstances are we responsible for any losses, direct or indirect, which are incurred as a result of the use of information contained within this document, including, but not limited to, errors, omissions, or inaccuracies.

Table of contents

Introduction 5
Chapter 1: 30-Day Meal Plan 6
Chapter 2: Breakfast and Brunch 9

Broccoli Frittata 9	Bacon with Eggs 17
German Pancakes 10	Omelet 18
Hash Browns 11	Fried Guacamole 19
Spinach Frittata 13	Crustless Mini Taco Quiche ... 21
Breakfast Biscuits 14	French Toast Sticks 22
Breakfast Bombs 15	Frittata 23
Tofu Scramble 16	

Chapter 3: Poultry 24

Thai Chili Fried Chicken Wings 24	Chicken Drumstick 32
Chicken Breast 26	Buttermilk Chicken 33
Naked Chicken Tenders 27	Lemon Pepper Chicken 34
Mediterranean Breaded Chicken 28	Chicken Fajita Rollups 35
Breaded Chicken Breasts 29	Caribbean Spiced Chicken ... 37
Fennel Chicken 30	Cornish Hens 38
Ranch Chicken Tenders 31	Tender Chicken Breasts 39

Chapter 4: Appetizers and Siders 40

Zucchini Strips 40	Mac and Cheese 49
Quiche 41	Spiced Okra Fries 50
Zucchini Fritters 42	Seasoned Rutabaga Fries 51
Patatas Bravas 43	Sweet Potato Cauliflower Patties 52
Latkes 44	Whole-Wheat Pizzas 53
Jicama Fries 45	Cauliflower Rice 54
Cauliflower 46	Turnip Fries 55
Zucchini, Yellow Squash, and Carrots 47	Chicken Nuggets 56
Cauliflower Fritters 48	

Chapter 5: Beef, Pork, and Lamb 57

Garlic Butter Pork Chops 57	Crispy Pork Chops 61
Southern Style Pork Chops . 58	Meatloaf Sliders 62
Beef and Mushroom Patties 59	Pork Dumplings with Dipping Sauce .63
Glazed Pork Tenderloin 60	Herbed Lamb Chops 65

Steak Nuggets 66
Italian-Style Meatballs 67
Rib Eye Steak 68
Pork Chops 69
Spicy Bacon Bites 70
Pork Chops with Brussels Sprouts 71
Spicy Lamb Steak 72

Chapter 6: Vegetarian 73

Roasted Rainbow Vegetables 73
Green Beans with Bacon 74
Yellow Squash 75
Falafel 76
Spaghetti Squash 78
Spaghetti Squash Fritters 79
Brussels Sprouts 80
Grilled Tomatoes 81
Veggie Quesadillas 82
Buttermilk Fried Mushrooms 83
Roasted Turnips 84
Artichoke Hearts 85
Ginger Soy Tofu 86
Loaded Potatoes 88
Cauliflower Wings 89
Brussels Sprouts 91
Eggplant 92

Chapter 7: Fish and Seafood 93

Fish Sticks 93
Lemon and Garlic Salmon 94
Blackened Fish Lettuce Wrap 95
Fish Skewers 96
Lemon Pepper Shrimp 98
Tomato Basil Scallops 99
Catfish with Green Beans 100
Garlic Lime Shrimp 101
Salmon and Asparagus 102
Fish Cakes with Cilantro 103
Pecan Crusted Halibut 104
Parmesan Shrimp 105
Cod 106
Salmon Cakes 107
Shrimp Scampi 108

Chapter 8: Dessert 109

Spiced Apples 109
Churros 110
Fruit Crumble Mug Cakes 112
Banana Bread 113
Apple Chips 114
Cheesecake Bites 115
Grilled Pineapple 116
Key Lime Cupcakes 117

Conclusion 118

Introduction

Eating low-fat food cooked in an air fryer will be good to your health. It reduces the risk of health conditions such as obesity, heart disease, heart attack and blocked arteries. So why not get a Mexican air fryer cookbook for your family?

With the Mexican Air Fryer Cookbook 2021 you can get the most from your air fryer to make a low-fat, and healthier way of cooking your favorite Mexican fried foods. The air fryer recipes equipped in this book was specially hand-picked and tried in our kitchen to produce near possible accurate results.

Whenever you crave for deep fried Mexican food, think of your healthy air fryer. Whenever you feel lazy to cook, think of how simple and fuss-free it is to cook healthy low-fat Mexican meals with your air fryer. With the air fryer cooker at home, no more salt and fat laden food to clog up your arteries! Say hello to guilt-free fried food.

Chapter 1: 30-Day Meal Plan

Day 1

Breakfast: German Pancakes

Lunch: Buffalo Chicken Wings

Dinner: Catfish With Green Beans

Dessert: Key Lime Cupcakes

Day 2

Breakfast: German Pancakes

Lunch: Buffalo Chicken Wings

Dinner: Catfish With Green Beans

Dessert: Key Lime Cupcakes

Day 3

Breakfast: German Pancakes

Lunch: Onion Rings

Dinner: Chicken Fajita Rollups

Dessert: Apple Chips

Day 4

Breakfast: German Pancakes

Lunch: Spicy Bacon Bites

Dinner: Cauliflower Rice

Dessert: Apple Chips

Day 5

Breakfast: Bacon with Eggs

Lunch: Brussels Sprouts

Dinner: Beef and Mushroom Patties

Dessert: Cheesecake Bites

Day 6

Breakfast: Bacon with Eggs

Lunch: Garlic Lime Shrimp

Dinner: Beef and Mushroom Patties

Dessert: Cheesecake Bites

Day 7

Breakfast: Frittata

Lunch: Chicken Drumstick

Dinner: Roasted Rainbow Vegetables

Dessert: Cheesecake Bites

Day 8

Breakfast: Frittata

Lunch: Spicy Lamb Steak

Dinner: Salmon Patties

Dessert: Grilled Pineapple

Day 9

Breakfast: Frittata

Lunch: Zucchini, Yellow Squash, and Carrots

Dinner: Salmon Patties

Dessert: Grilled Pineapple

Day 10

Breakfast: Frittata

Lunch: Steak Nuggets

Dinner: Lemon Pepper Chicken

Dessert: Churros

Day 11

Breakfast: Fried Guacamole

Lunch: Steak Nuggets

Dinner: Lemon Pepper Chicken

Dessert: Churros

Day 12

Breakfast: Fried Guacamole

Lunch: Green Beans with Bacon

Dinner: Italian-Style Meatballs

Dessert: Churros

Day 13

Breakfast: Hash Browns

Lunch: Scotch Eggs

Dinner: Italian-Style Meatballs

Dessert: Spiced Apples

Day 14

Breakfast: Hash Browns

Lunch: Green Beans with Bacon

Dinner: Ginger Soy Tofu

Dessert: Spiced Apples

Day 15

Breakfast: Hash Browns

Lunch: Fish Sticks

Dinner: Ginger Soy Tofu

Dessert: Banana Bread

Day 16

Breakfast: Hash Browns

Lunch: Fish Sticks

Dinner: Shrimp Scampi

Dessert: Banana Bread

Day 17

Breakfast: Breakfast Biscuits

Lunch: Thai Chili Fried Chicken Wings

Dinner: Shrimp Scampi

Dessert: Banana Bread

Day 18

Breakfast: Breakfast Biscuits

Lunch: Thai Chili Fried Chicken Wings

Dinner: Caribbean Spiced Chicken

Dessert: Banana Bread

Day 19

Breakfast: Breakfast Biscuits

Lunch: Sweet Potato Cauliflower Patties

Dinner: Caribbean Spiced Chicken

Dessert: Fruit Crumble Mug Cakes

Day 20

Breakfast: Breakfast Biscuits

Lunch: Sweet Potato Cauliflower Patties

Dinner: Meatloaf Sliders

Dessert: Fruit Crumble Mug Cakes

Day 21

Breakfast: Tofu Scramble

Lunch: Steak Bites and Mushrooms

Dinner: Veggie Quesadillas

Dessert: Fruit Crumble Mug Cakes

Day 22

Breakfast: Tofu Scramble

Lunch: Steak Bites and Mushrooms

Dinner: Tomato Basil Scallops

Dessert: Fruit Crumble Mug Cakes

Day 23

Breakfast: French Toast Sticks

Lunch: Loaded Potatoes

Dinner: Mediterranean Breaded Chicken

Dessert: Apple Chips

Day 24

Breakfast: French Toast Sticks

Lunch: Salmon and Asparagus

Dinner: Rib Eye Steak

Dessert: Apple Chips

Day 25

Breakfast: French Toast Sticks

Lunch: Salmon and Asparagus

Dinner: Parmesan Shrimp

Dessert: Key Lime Cupcakes

Day 26

Breakfast: French Toast Sticks

Lunch: Chicken Breast

Dinner: Fennel Chicken

Dessert: Key Lime Cupcakes

Day 27

Breakfast: Breakfast Bombs

Lunch: Mac and Cheese

Dinner: Pork Dumplings with Dipping Sauce

Dessert: Grilled Pineapple

Day 28

Breakfast: Breakfast Bombs

Lunch: Whole-Wheat Pizzas

Dinner: Herbed Lamb Chops

Dessert: Grilled Pineapple

Day 29

Breakfast: Omelet

Lunch: Falafel

Dinner: Herbed Lamb Chops

Dessert: Banana Bread

Day 30

Breakfast: Omelet

Lunch: Pork Chops

Dinner: Tso's Chicken

Dessert: Banana Bread

Chapter 2: Breakfast and Brunch

Broccoli Frittata

Preparation time: 5 minutes
Cooking time: 17 minutes
Servings: 4

Ingredients:

- ½ cup chopped broccoli florets
- ½ teaspoon salt
- ½ cup chopped bell pepper
- ¼ teaspoon ground black pepper
- 2 tablespoons almond milk, unsweetened
- 3 eggs
- 2 tablespoons grated parmesan cheese

Method:

1. Switch on the air fryer, insert fryer basket, then shut with its lid, set the fryer at 350 degrees F, and preheat for 5 minutes.
2. Meanwhile, take a heatproof dish, grease it with oil and then place bell peppers and florets in it.
3. Open the fryer, arrange the dish in the air fryer basket, close with its lid and cook for 7 minutes.
4. In the meantime, take a medium bowl, crack the eggs in it, add salt, black pepper and milk and then whisk until blended.
5. When the vegetables have cooked, pour the egg mixture over the vegetables, sprinkle cheese on top and then continue cooking for 10 minutes.
6. When the air fryer beeps, open its lid, take out the dish, cut frittata into slices and then serve.

Nutrition Value:

- Calories: 171 Cal
- Fat: 20.6 g
- Carbs: 5.6 g
- Protein: 16 g
- Fiber: 1.1 g

German Pancakes

Preparation time: 10 minutes
Cooking time: 18 minutes
Servings: 5

Ingredients:

- 1 cup oat flour
- 1/16 teaspoon salt
- 2 tablespoons olive oil
- 3 eggs
- 1 cup coconut milk, unsweetened
- Fresh berries, as needed for garnishing
- Swerve confectioners' sugar, as needed for garnish

Method:

1. Switch on the air fryer, insert fryer basket, then shut with its lid, set the fryer at 390 degrees F, and preheat for 10 minutes.
2. Meanwhile, place all the ingredients in a blender, except for garnishing ones, and pulse until smooth; add 1 tablespoon of coconut milk if the batter is too thick.
3. Take a heatproof ramekin, grease it with olive oil, then pour in pancake batter and spread it evenly.
4. Open the fryer, add ramekin in it, close with its lid and cook for 6 to 8 minutes until the pancake has cooked and the top is golden brown.
5. When air fryer beeps, open its lid, take out the ramekin, then top with berries, and sprinkle with swerve confectioners' and serve.

Nutrition Value:

- Calories: 139 Cal
- Fat: 4 g
- Carbs: 18 g
- Protein: 8 g
- Fiber: 3 g

Hash Browns

Preparation time: 30 minutes
Cooking time: 35 minutes |
Servings: 2

Ingredients:

- 1 small red onion, peeled, 1-inch sliced
- 1 1/2 pounds potatoes, peeled
- 1 medium red bell pepper, deseeded, 1-inch cubed
- 1 jalapeno, deseeded, cut into 1-inch rings
- 1/8 teaspoon salt
- 1/2 teaspoon ground cumin
- 1/8 teaspoon ground black pepper
- 1/2 teaspoon taco seasoning mix
- 1 1/2 tablespoon olive oil

Method:

1. Cut potatoes into 1-inch cubes, place them in a bowl, cover them with chilled water and let soak for 20 minutes.
2. Then switch on the air fryer, insert fryer basket, grease it with olive oil, then shut with its lid, set the fryer at 320 degrees F, and preheat for 5 minutes.
3. Meanwhile, drain the potatoes, pat dry with paper towels, place them in a bowl, drizzle with 1 tablespoon oil and toss until coated.
4. Open the fryer, add potatoes in it, close with its lid and cook for 18 minutes until nicely golden, shaking the basket every 5 minutes.
5. In the meantime, add onion, bell pepper, and jalapeno into the bowl that was used for potatoes, drizzle remaining oil over vegetables, season with salt, taco seasoning, black pepper, and cumin and toss until well coated.
6. When potatoes are done, add them to the bowl containing vegetable mixture and toss until mixed.
7. Return fryer basket into the air fryer, grease it with olive oil, then shut with its lid, set the fryer at 356 degrees F, and preheat for 5 minutes.
8. Then open the fryer, add the vegetable mixture in it, close with its lid and cook for 12 minutes until nicely golden and crispy, shaking the basket every 5 minutes.
9. When air fryer beeps, open its lid, transfer hash browns onto a serving plate and serve.

Nutrition Value:

- Calories: 186 Cal
- Fat: 4.3 g
- Carbs: 4 g
- Protein: 4 g
- Fiber: 4.8 g

Spinach Frittata

Preparation time: 5 minutes
Cooking time: 10 minutes
Servings: 4

Ingredients:

- 1 green onion, chopped
- ½ cup spinach leaves
- 2 tablespoons diced red bell pepper
- 1/8 teaspoon cayenne pepper
- 4 eggs
- ½ cup shredded cheese

Method:

1. Switch on the air fryer, insert fryer basket, grease it with non-stick cooking oil spray, then shut with its lid, set the fryer at 390 degrees F, and preheat for 5 minutes.
2. Meanwhile, take a large bowl, place all the ingredients in it, whisk until combined and then spoon the mixture into a heatproof dish greased with oil.
3. Open the fryer, arrange the prepared dish in the air fryer basket, close with its lid and cook for 10 minutes until thoroughly cooked.
4. Serve straight away.

Nutrition Value:

- Calories: 194 Cal
- Fat: 11.2 g
- Carbs: 4.1 g
- Protein: 12.8 g
- Fiber: 1.4 g

Breakfast Biscuits

Preparation time: 10 minutes
Cooking time: 15 minutes
Servings: 9

Ingredients:

- 1 cup almond flour
- 1/4 teaspoon sea salt
- 1/2 teaspoon baking powder
- 2 tablespoons butter, melted
- 2 tablespoons sour cream, non-fat
- 1 cup shredded cheddar cheese, non-fat
- 2 organic eggs

Method:

1. Place flour in a bowl, add salt and baking powder, stir until just mixed and then stir cheese by hand until incorporated.
2. Crack eggs in another bowl, whisk in butter and sour cream until blended, and then slowly stir this mixture with a large fork until sticky batter comes together.
3. Switch on the air fryer, then shut with its lid, set the fryer at 220 degrees F, and preheat for 5 minutes.
4. Meanwhile, take a fryer basket, line it with parchment sheet, and then drop scoops of prepared biscuit batter in a single layer, about ¼ cup of batter for large biscuits or 2 tablespoons of batter for small biscuits.
5. Open the fryer, insert fryer basket in it, close with its lid and cook for 10 minutes for large or 6 minutes for small biscuits until nicely golden and thoroughly cooked.
6. When air fryer beeps, open its lid, transfer biscuits onto a serving plate and serve.

Nutrition Value:

- Calories: 167 Cal
- Fat: 15 g
- Carbs: 3 g
- Protein: 7 g
- Fiber: 1 g

Breakfast Bombs

Preparation time: 10 minutes
Cooking time: 40 minutes
Servings: 4

Ingredients:

- 4 ounces whole-wheat pizza dough
- 3 slices of bacon, center-cut
- 1 tablespoon chopped fresh chives
- 3 large eggs, beaten
- 1-ounce cream cheese, softened, low-fat

Method:

1. Take a skillet pan, place it over medium heat, add bacon, and cook for 10 minutes until very crispy.
2. Then transfer bacon to a cutting board, let it cool for 3 minutes and then crumble it, set aside until required.
3. Pour beaten eggs into the skillet pan, stir and cook for 1 minute until eggs are almost set.
4. Transfer eggs into a bowl, add bacon, chives, and cream cheese and stir well until combined.
5. Switch on the air fryer, insert fryer basket, grease it with olive oil, then shut with its lid, set the fryer at 350 degrees F, and preheat for 5 minutes.
6. Meanwhile, divide pizza dough into four sections, roll each section into the 5-inch round crust, and then add one-fourth of the cooked egg mixture into the center of each crust.
7. Brush the edges of the crust with water and then form a purse by wrapping crust around the egg mixture.
8. Open the fryer, add crust in it in a single layer, then spray with olive oil, close with its lid and cook for 6 minutes until nicely golden brown.
9. When air fryer beeps, open its lid, transfer the breakfast bomb onto a serving plate and cook the remaining crust in the same manner.
10. Serve straight away.

Nutrition Value:

- Calories: 305 Cal
- Fat: 15 g
- Carbs: 26 g
- Protein: 19 g
- Fiber: 2 g

Tofu Scramble

Preparation time: 10 minutes
Cooking time: 30 minutes
Servings: 3

Ingredients:

- 4 cups broccoli florets
- 1 block tofu, drained, pressed, 1-inch cubed
- 2 1/2 cups chopped red potato, 1-inch cubed
- 1/2 cup chopped red onion
- 1/2 teaspoon garlic powder
- 1/2 teaspoon onion powder
- 1 teaspoon ground turmeric
- 2 tablespoons soy sauce
- 2 tablespoons olive oil

Method:

1. Place tofu pieces in a bowl, add onion, onion powder, garlic powder, and turmeric, drizzle with 1 tablespoon olive oil and soy sauce, toss until well coated, and set aside to marinate until required.
2. Switch on the air fryer, insert fryer basket, grease it with olive oil, then shut with its lid, set the fryer at 400 degrees F, and preheat for 5 minutes.
3. Meanwhile, place potato pieces in a bowl, add remaining oil and toss until well coated.
4. Open the fryer, add potatoes pieces in it, close with its lid and cook for 15 minutes until nicely golden and crispy, shaking the basket every 5 minutes.
5. Then add marinated tofu pieces into the fryer basket, shake well, reserving the marinade, and continue cooking for 10 minutes at 370 degrees F, shaking the basket every 5 minutes.
6. In the meantime, add broccoli florets into the reserved marinade, toss until coated, and set aside until required.
7. After 10 minutes of frying, add broccoli into fryer basket, shake well to mix and cook for 5 minutes
8. When air fryer beeps, open its lid, transfer tofu, potatoes, and broccoli florets onto a serving plate and serve.

Nutrition Value:

- Calories: 276.3 Cal
- Fat: 12.3 g
- Carbs: 29 g
- Protein: 13.1 g
- Fiber: 5 g

Bacon with Eggs

Preparation time: 5 minutes
Cooking time: 23 minutes
Servings: 1

Ingredients:

- 2 slices of bacon, thick-cut
- 2 eggs
- ¼ teaspoon salt
- ¼ teaspoon ground black pepper
- 2 tablespoons unsalted butter

Method:

1. Switch on the air fryer, insert fryer basket, grease it with olive oil, then shut with its lid, set the fryer at 400 degrees F, and preheat for 5 minutes.
2. Then open the fryer, add bacon slices in it in a single layer, close with its lid and cook for 10 minutes until crispy and done, shaking the basket every 5 minutes.
3. When air fryer beeps, open its lid, transfer bacon onto a serving plate and set aside until required.
4. Replace fryer basket with air fryer baking pan, add butter in it, then shut with its lid, set the fryer at 400 degrees F, and cook for 1 minute until the butter has melted.
5. Crack eggs in the baking pan, switch temperature to 325 degrees F, close air fryer with lid and cook for 6 to 8 minutes or until eggs are fried to the desired level.
6. When air fryer beeps, open its lid, transfer fried eggs onto a serving plate and serve with bacon.

Nutrition Value:

- Calories: 487 Cal
- Fat: 44.4 g
- Carbs: 1.2 g
- Protein: 20.7 g
- Fiber: 0 g

Omelet

Preparation time: 5 minutes
Cooking time: 15 minutes
Servings: 1

Ingredients:

- 2 tablespoons chopped ham
- 2 tablespoons chopped red bell pepper
- 2 tablespoons sliced green onion
- 1 tablespoon chopped mushroom
- ¼ teaspoon salt
- 1 teaspoon breakfast seasoning
- 2 eggs
- ¼ cup coconut milk, unsweetened
- 2 tablespoons grated cheddar cheese
- 2 tablespoons grated mozzarella cheese

Method:

1. Switch on the air fryer, insert fryer baking pan, grease it with olive oil, then shut with its lid, set the fryer at 350 degrees F, and preheat for 5 minutes.
2. Meanwhile, place crack eggs in a bowl, whisk them until beaten, then add ham, pepper, onion, mushrooms, and salt and whisk until just mixed.
3. Open the fryer, pour in egg mixture, close with its lid and cook for 5 minutes.
4. Then sprinkle breakfast seasoning on top, scatter with cheeses and continue cooking for 5 minutes until cheese has melted and omelet has cooked.
5. When air fryer beeps, open its lid, take out the baking pan, slide omelet onto a serving plate and serve.

Nutrition Value:

- Calories: 350 Cal
- Fat: 16 g
- Carbs: 19 g
- Protein: 6 g
- Fiber: 2 g

Fried Guacamole

Preparation time: 6 hours and 15 minutes
Cooking time: 16 minutes
Servings: 10

Ingredients:

- 1/3 cup almond flour
- 1 egg

- 1 1/2 cups panko bread crumbs
- 1 egg white

For Guacamole:

- 3 medium avocados, halved, pitted, peeled
- 1/3 cup chopped cilantro
- 1/3 cup chopped red onion
- ½ teaspoon ground black pepper

- 2 teaspoons ground cumin
- 1 teaspoon of sea salt
- 8 tablespoons almond flour
- 1 lime, juiced

Method:

1. Prepare guacamole and for this, take a bowl, add all its ingredients in it except for flour and mash with a fork until well combined.
2. Gradually mix the flour until thick and brownie dough-like batter comes together and freeze for 1 to 2 hours until the mixture has hardened.
3. Meanwhile, take a baking sheet, and then line it with aluminum foil.
4. After 2 hours, use a spoon to scoop out guacamole, shape it into a ball, and then place onto the prepared baking sheet.
5. Prepare remaining guacamole balls in the same manner, cover the balls with aluminum foil, and then freeze for a minimum of 4 hours or overnight.
6. Then switch on the air fryer, insert fryer basket, grease it with olive oil, then shut with its lid, set the fryer at 220 degrees F, and preheat for 5 minutes.
7. In the meantime, crack the egg in a bowl, add egg white and whisk until combined.
8. Place bread crumbs in a shallow dish and then place almond flour in another shallow dish.
9. Working on one guacamole ball at a time, first spray the ball with oil, then coat with almond flour, dip into the egg mixture, then dredge with parmesan cheese and place the ball into heated fryer basket.

10. Fill the fryer basket with more guacamole balls in the single layer, spray with olive oil, close with its lid and cook for 8 minutes until nicely golden and crispy, shaking the basket halfway through.
11. When air fryer beeps, open its lid, transfer guacamole balls onto a serving plate, cook remaining guacamole balls in the same manner and serve.

Nutrition Value:

- Calories: 179 Cal
- Fat: 13 g
- Carbs: 14 g
- Protein: 6 g
- Fiber: 6 g

Crustless Mini Taco Quiche

Preparation time: 10 minutes
Cooking time: 28 minutes
Servings: 4

Ingredients:

- 1 medium green bell pepper, cored, diced
- ½ pound ground pork
- 1 small red onion, peeled, diced
- ½ pound ground beef
- 1 medium red bell pepper, cored, diced
- 1 teaspoon salt
- 2 tablespoons taco seasoning
- 1 teaspoon ground black pepper
- ¼ cup tomato salsa
- ¼ cup vegan heavy cream
- 4 eggs
- 1 cup shredded Mexican blend cheese

Method:

1. Take a medium skillet pan, place it over medium-high heat and when hot, add ground pork and beef.
2. Stir in salt and black pepper, and then cook the meat for 8 to 10 minutes until nicely browned.
3. Add onion and bell peppers, stir in taco seasoning and continue cooking the meat for 4 minutes until vegetables turn soft.
4. Meanwhile, take a large bowl, crack the eggs in it, add salsa, cream and cheese and then whisk until well combined.
5. Take four mini pie pans, grease them with oil, evenly fill the pans with the cooked meat mixture and then cover with the egg mixture.
6. Switch on the air fryer, insert fryer basket, then shut with its lid, set the fryer at 350 degrees F, and preheat for 5 minutes.
7. Open the fryer, arrange pie pans in the air fryer basket in a single layer, close with its lid and cook for 12 minutes until thoroughly cooked.
8. Serve straight away.

Nutrition Value:

- Calories: 100 Cal
- Fat: 100 g
- Carbs: 100 g
- Protein: 100 g
- Fiber: 100 g

French Toast Sticks

Preparation time: 10 minutes
Cooking time: 17 minutes
Servings: 2

Ingredients:

- 4 slices of almond bread
- 1/16 teaspoon salt
- 1/16 teaspoon ground cloves
- 1/16 teaspoon ground cinnamon
- 1 teaspoon Swerve icing sugar
- 1/16 teaspoon nutmeg
- 2 tablespoons unsalted butter, softened
- 2 eggs, lightly beaten

Method:

1. Crack the eggs in a bowl, whisk until beaten, then add salt, cloves, cinnamon, and nutmeg, and whisk until mixed.
2. Switch on the air fryer, insert fryer basket, grease it with olive oil, then shut with its lid, set the fryer at 350 degrees F, and preheat for 5 minutes.
3. Meanwhile, spread butter on both sides of bread slices, cut the slices into strips and then dredge into the egg batter.
4. Open the fryer, add bread strips in it in a single layer, spray with olive oil, close with its lid and cook for 6 minutes until nicely golden and crispy, flipping and spraying with oil halfway through.
5. When air fryer beeps, open its lid, transfer French toasts onto a serving plate and cook remaining bread strips in the same manner.
6. When done, sprinkle Swerve icing sugar on the French toasts and serve.

Nutrition Value:

- Calories: 178 Cal
- Fat: 15 g
- Carbs: 2 g
- Protein: 5 g
- Fiber: 0.5 g

Frittata

Preparation time: 10 minutes
Cooking time: 14 minutes
Servings: 2

Ingredients:

- 1 ½ stick of Chinese waxed sausage, sliced lengthwise
- ¼ cup chopped kale
- ¼ cup baby spinach leaves
- 2 tablespoons corn
- 1 tablespoon chopped red onion
- 2 tablespoons peas
- 1 small green bell pepper, cored, julienne cut
- 1 medium carrot, peeled, julienne cut
- 1/8 teaspoon salt
- 1/8 teaspoon ground black pepper
- ¼ teaspoon olive oil
- 3 eggs

Method:

1. Switch on the air fryer, then shut with its lid, set the fryer at 350 degrees F, and preheat for 5 minutes.
2. Meanwhile, grease the air fryer baking pan, place sausage in it, add onion, stir until just mixed and spread evenly.
3. Open the fryer, insert baking pan in it, close with its lid and cook for 4 minutes.
4. Meanwhile, place the remaining ingredients in a bowl and whisk well until combined.
5. When air fryer beeps, open its lid, pour in the prepared batter, and continue cooking for 4 minutes.
6. Then increase air frying temperature to 390 degrees F and cook for 1 minute until the top of the frittata is nicely browned.
7. When air fryer beeps, open its lid, take out the baking pan, transfer frittata onto a serving plate, then cut it into slices and serve.

Nutrition Value:

- Calories: 290.5 Cal
- Fat: 19.7 g
- Carbs: 11 g
- Protein: 17.4 g
- Fiber: 2 g

Chapter 3: Poultry

Thai Chili Fried Chicken Wings

Preparation time: 40 minutes
Cooking time: 30 minutes
Servings: 2

Ingredients:

- 16 chicken wings
- 1/2 cup almond flour
- 2 ½ teaspoons chicken seasoning
- 1/4 cup buttermilk, low-fat

For Thai Chili Marinade:

- 2 green onions, chopped
- 1 teaspoon grated ginger
- 1 ½ teaspoon minced garlic
- 1 teaspoon honey
- 3 tablespoons soy sauce
- 1 teaspoon of rice wine vinegar
- 1 tablespoon Sriracha sauce
- 1 tablespoon sesame oil

Method:

1. Prepare the marinade, and for this, place all its ingredients in a blender and pulse for 1 minute until blended.
2. Pat dry chicken wings, place them in a large plastic bag, pour in the buttermilk, then add chicken seasoning, seal the bag, turn it upside down until chicken wings have coated, and then marinate in the refrigerator for a minimum of 30 minutes.
3. Once the chicken wings have marinated, switch on the air fryer, insert fryer basket, grease it with olive oil, then shut with its lid, set the fryer at 400 degrees F, and preheat for 5 minutes.
4. Meanwhile, place flour in another plastic bag, add marinated chicken wings in it, then seal the bag and shake until chicken wings have evenly coated with almond flour.
5. Open the fryer, stack chicken wings in it, spray with olive oil, close with its lid and cook for 15 minutes until nicely golden and thoroughly cooked, shaking the basket every 5 minutes and flipping the chicken wings halfway through.
6. When air fryer beeps, open its lid, take out the chicken wings and brush well with the prepared marinade.
7. Return chicken wings into the air fryer, shut with lid, and continue cooking for 7 to 10 minutes until glazed.

8. Serve straight away.

Nutrition Value:

- Calories: 202 Cal
- Fat: 11 g
- Carbs: 12 g
- Protein: 12 g
- Fiber: 2 g

Chicken Breast

Preparation time: 5 minutes
Cooking time: 15 minutes
Servings: 1

Ingredients:

- 7 ounces chicken breast, skinless
- 1 teaspoon chicken seasoning
- 2 teaspoons olive oil
- Mediterranean salad for serving

Method:

1. Switch on the air fryer, insert fryer basket, grease it with olive oil, then shut with its lid, set the fryer at 390 degrees F, and preheat for 5 minutes.
2. Meanwhile, coat chicken with oil and then season them with chicken seasoning on both sides.
3. Open the fryer, add chicken breasts in it, close with its lid and cook for 15 minutes until nicely golden and thoroughly cooked, shaking the basket every 5 minutes and flipping the chicken breast halfway through.
4. When air fryer beeps, open its lid, transfer chicken breast onto a cutting board, let it cool for 5 minutes and then cut it into slices.
5. Serve chicken with Mediterranean salad.

Nutrition Value:

- Calories: 262 Cal
- Fat: 6 g
- Carbs: 1 g
- Protein: 48 g
- Fiber: 0 g

Naked Chicken Tenders

Preparation time: 5 minutes
Cooking time: 15 minutes
Servings: 4

Ingredients:

- 6 chicken tenders, skinless
- 1 teaspoon garlic powder
- 1 teaspoon salt
- 1 teaspoon onion powder
- 1 teaspoon dried oregano
- 1 teaspoon paprika

Method:

1. Switch on the air fryer, insert fryer basket, grease it with non-stick cooking oil spray, then shut with its lid, set the fryer at 380 degrees F, and preheat for 5 minutes.
2. Meanwhile, take a resealable plastic bag
3. place chicken tenders in it and then add the remaining ingredients.
4. Seal the bag and then turn it upside down until chicken tenders are coated in the seasonings.
5. Open the fryer, arrange the chicken tenders in the air fryer basket in a single layer, spray oil on the food, close with its lid and cook for 13 to 15 minutes until thoroughly cooked and golden brown, turning halfway.
6. Serve straight away.

Nutrition Value:

- Calories: 200 Cal
- Fat: 4 g
- Carbs: 12.9 g
- Protein: 27.7 g
- Fiber: 2.3 g

Mediterranean Breaded Chicken

Preparation time: 10 minutes
Cooking time: 30 minutes
Servings: 2

Ingredients:

- 2 large chicken breast, cut into nugget-style pieces
- ½ teaspoon salt
- 1 tablespoon dried thyme
- ½ teaspoon ground black pepper
- 3 ounces Tuscan herb granola
- 1 egg

Method:

1. Switch on the air fryer, insert fryer basket, grease it with olive oil, then shut with its lid, set the fryer at 350 degrees F, and preheat for 10 minutes.
2. Meanwhile, crack the egg in a bowl, whisk it until beaten and set aside until required.
3. Take granola in a plastic bag, seal it and then bash it with a rolling pin until the mixture resembles medium pieces.
4. Add salt, thyme, and black pepper into the granola, seal the bag and shake it until mixed.
5. Coat chicken pieces in the egg, then add them into the granola mixture, seal the bag and shake it until chicken pieces are evenly coated.
6. Open the fryer, add chicken nuggets in it in a single layer, spray with oil, close with its lid and cook for 20 minutes until nicely golden and crispy, shaking the basket every 5 minutes.
7. When air fryer beeps, open its lid, transfer chicken nuggets onto a serving plate and serve.

Nutrition Value:

- Calories: 453.5 Cal
- Fat: 17.1 g
- Carbs: 22.7 g
- Protein: 52.2 g
- Fiber: 2.7 g

Breaded Chicken Breasts

Preparation time: 10 minutes
Cooking time: 22 minutes
Servings: 4

Ingredients:

- 1 pound chicken breast, skinless, pounded
- 1 teaspoon salt
- 1 cup oats
- 1 teaspoon ground black pepper
- 1 cup almond flour
- 1 egg

Method:

1. Switch on the air fryer, insert fryer basket, grease it with non-stick cooking oil spray, then shut with its lid, set the fryer at 390 degrees F, and preheat for 5 minutes.
2. Meanwhile, take a shallow dish, place flour in it, add ½ teaspoon each of salt and black pepper and then stir until mixed.
3. Take a medium bowl, crack the egg in it and then whisk until blended.
4. Take a separate shallow dish, place oats in it, add remaining salt and black pepper and then stir until mixed.
5. Working on each chicken breast at a time, dredge into the almond flour mixture, dip into the egg and then dredge into the oats mixture until coated.
6. Open the fryer, arrange the prepared chicken breasts in the air fryer basket in a single layer, spray oil on the food, close with its lid and cook for 22 minutes until thoroughly cooked, turning halfway.
7. Serve straight away.

Nutrition Value:

- Calories: 393 Cal
- Fat: 5.1 g
- Carbs: 49.2 g
- Protein: 34.5 g
- Fiber: 0.2 g

Fennel Chicken

Preparation time: 40 minutes
Cooking time: 35 minutes
Servings: 4

Ingredients:

- 1 pound chicken thighs, boneless, skinless
- 1 large red onion, peeled, 1-1/2 inch sliced
- 2 teaspoons lemon juice
- 1/4 cup chopped cilantro

For Marinade:

- 2 teaspoons minced ginger
- 2 teaspoons minced garlic
- 1 teaspoon salt
- 1 teaspoon cayenne pepper
- 1 teaspoon turmeric
- 1 teaspoon smoked paprika
- 1 teaspoon garam masala
- 1 teaspoon ground fennel seeds
- 1 tablespoon olive oil

Method:

1. Prepare the marinade and for this, place all its ingredients in a large bowl and stir until combined.
2. Pierce chicken thighs with a fork, then add to marinade along with onion, toss until well coated and marinate for a minimum of 30 minutes in the refrigerator.
3. When chicken and vegetables have marinated, switch on the air fryer, insert fryer basket, grease it with olive oil, then shut with its lid, set the fryer at 360 degrees F, and preheat for 5 minutes.
4. Open the fryer, add chicken and onions in it, spray with olive oil, close with its lid and cook for 15 minutes until nicely golden and cooked, shaking the basket every 5 minutes.
5. When air fryer beeps, open its lid, transfer chicken and vegetables onto a serving plate, drizzle with lemon juice, sprinkle with cilantro, and serve.

Nutrition Value:

- Calories: 190 Cal
- Fat: 100 g
- Carbs: 100 g
- Protein: 100 g
- Fiber: 100 g

Ranch Chicken Tenders

Preparation time: 10 minutes
Cooking time: 25 minutes
Servings: 8

Ingredients:

- 14 ounces chicken tenders, skinless
- 2 tablespoons almond flour
- 2/3 cup oats
- ¼ teaspoon salt
- 2 teaspoons chicken seasoning
- ¼ teaspoon ground black pepper
- 1/3 cup ranch dressing
- ½ cup vegan shredded cheddar cheese

Method:

1. Switch on the air fryer, insert fryer basket, line it with parchment sheet, grease it with non-stick cooking oil spray, then shut with its lid, set the fryer at 325 degrees F, and preheat for 5 minutes.
2. Meanwhile, take a shallow dish, almond flour in it, add chicken seasoning and then stir until combined.
3. Take a separate shallow dish, oats in it, add salt and black pepper and then stir until combined.
4. Take a separate shallow dish and then place the ranch dressing in it.
5. Working on one chicken tender at a time, dredge it in almond flour mixture, dip into the ranch dressing
6. and dredge into the oat mixture until well-coated.
7. Open the fryer, arrange chicken tenders in the air fryer basket in a single layer, spray oil on the food, close with its lid and cook for 20 to 25 minutes until thoroughly cooked and golden brown, turning halfway.
8. Serve straight away.

Nutrition Value:

- Calories: 150 Cal
- Fat: 7 g
- Carbs: 9 g
- Protein: 13 g
- Fiber: 2 g

Chicken Drumstick

Preparation time: 10 minutes
Cooking time: 25 minutes
Servings: 4

Ingredients:

- 2 1/2 pounds chicken drumsticks
- 1/4 cup coconut flour
- 1/2 teaspoon garlic powder
- 1/2 teaspoon sea salt
- 1 teaspoon smoked paprika
- 1/4 teaspoon ground black pepper
- 1/4 teaspoon dried thyme
- 2 large eggs
- 1 cup pork rinds

Method:

1. Place coconut flour in a shallow dish, add salt and black pepper and stir until mixed.
2. Crack eggs in another dish and then whisk until beaten.
3. Place pork rinds in another dish, add garlic, thyme, and pork rinds and stir until mixed.
4. Switch on the air fryer, insert fryer basket, grease it with olive oil, then shut with its lid, set the fryer at 400 degrees F, and preheat for 5 minutes.
5. Meanwhile, first coat chicken drumsticks into the coconut flour mixture, then dip into the eggs and dredge into pork rind mixture until evenly coated.
6. Open the fryer, add chicken drumsticks in it in a single layer, spray with olive oil, close with its lid and cook for 20 minutes until crispy and cooked, shaking the basket every 5 minutes.
7. When air fryer beeps, open its lid, transfer chicken drumsticks onto a serving plate, and cooking remaining drumsticks in the same manner.
8. Serve straight away.

Nutrition Value:

- Calories: 273 Cal
- Fat: 15 g
- Carbs: 3 g
- Protein: 28 g
- Fiber: 1 g

Buttermilk Chicken

Preparation time: 10 minutes
Cooking time: 15 minutes
Servings: 6

Ingredients:

- 1 ½ pound boneless, skinless chicken thighs
- 1 cup oats
- 1 cup almond flour
- ½ tablespoon ground black pepper
- 1 tablespoon seasoned salt
- 2 cups buttermilk

Method:

1. Take a large bowl, place chicken thighs in it, add buttermilk and then let the chicken rest in the refrigerator for a minimum of 4 hours.
2. Then switch on the air fryer, insert fryer basket, grease it with non-stick cooking oil spray, then shut with its lid, set the fryer at 380 degrees F, and preheat for 5 minutes.
3. Meanwhile, take a large plastic bag
4. place almond flour in it, add salt and black pepper and then add chicken thighs.
5. Seal the bag and then turn it upside down until chicken thighs are coated in flour.
6. Take a shallow dish and then place oats in it.
7. Working on chicken thigh at a time, dip into buttermilk and then dredge in oats until well coated.
8. Open the fryer, arrange prepared chicken thighs in the air fryer basket in a single layer, spray oil on the food, close with its lid and cook for 15 minutes until thoroughly cooked and golden brown, turning halfway.
9. Serve straight away.

Nutrition Value:

- Calories: 335 Cal
- Fat: 12.8 g
- Carbs: 33.2 g
- Protein: 24.5 g
- Fiber: 0.8 g

Lemon Pepper Chicken

Preparation time: 10 minutes
Cooking time: 19 minutes
Servings: 6

Ingredients:

- 6 large skinless chicken breasts
- 3 tablespoons lemon pepper seasoning
- 2 teaspoons Worcestershire sauce
- 1 teaspoon salt
- ¼ cup lemon juice
- ¼ cup olive oil

Method:

1. Cut chicken into bite-size pieces, add them into a large bowl, then add remaining ingredients, stir until well coated, and let marinate for a minimum in the refrigerator.
2. When the chicken has marinated, switch on the air fryer, insert fryer basket, grease it with olive oil, then shut with its lid, set the fryer at 350 degrees F, and preheat for 5 minutes.
3. Open the fryer, add chicken pieces in it, close with its lid and cook for 14 minutes until nicely golden and cooked through, shaking the basket every 5 minutes, flipping chicken and spraying with oil halfway.
4. When air fryer beeps, open its lid, transfer chicken onto a serving plate and serve.

Nutrition Value:

- Calories: 149.4 Cal
- Fat: 1.7 g
- Carbs: 3.2 g
- Protein: 29.6 g
- Fiber: 0.9 g

Chicken Fajita Rollups

Preparation time: 15 minutes
Cooking time: 17 minutes
Servings: 6

Ingredients:

- 1/2 of large yellow bell pepper, cored, cut into strips
- 3 large chicken breasts
- 1/2 of large red bell pepper, cored, cut into strips
- 1/2 large red onion, peeled, sliced
- 1/2 of large green bell pepper, cored, cut into strips

For Spice Mix:

- 1 teaspoon garlic powder
- 2 teaspoons paprika
- ¾ teaspoon salt
- 1 teaspoon cumin powder
- 1/2 teaspoon cayenne pepper
- ¼ teaspoon ground black pepper
- 1/2 teaspoon dried oregano

Method:

1. Prepare spice mix and for this, place all its ingredients in a bowl and stir until mixed, set aside until required.
2. Slice each chicken breast in half lengthwise, then cover each chicken slice in a plastic wrap or place it between two parchment papers and pound with a meat mallet until ¼-inch thick.
3. Prepare rolls and for this, season both sides of chicken breast with prepare spice mix, then divide six strips of bell peppers of each color and onion slices on one side of chicken, then roll tightly and secure with a toothpick.
4. Then switch on the air fryer, insert fryer basket, grease it with olive oil, then shut with its lid, set the fryer at 400 degrees F, and preheat for 5 minutes.
5. Open the fryer, add chicken rolls in it, spray them with olive oil, close with its lid and cook for 12 minutes until nicely golden and cooked thoroughly, shaking the basket every 5 minutes and turning rolls halfway.
6. When air fryer beeps, open its lid, transfer chicken fajita rolls onto a serving plate and serve.

Nutrition Value:

- Calories: 138.2 Cal
- Fat: 3.4 g
- Carbs: 4.1 g
- Protein: 22.8 g
- Fiber: 1.2 g

Caribbean Spiced Chicken

Preparation time: 10 minutes
Cooking time: 25 minutes
Servings: 8

Ingredients:

- 3 pounds chicken thigh, boneless, skinless
- 1 1/2 teaspoons ground ginger
- 1 tablespoon ground cinnamon
- 1 ½ teaspoon salt
- 1 tablespoon cayenne pepper
- 1 tablespoon ground coriander
- 1 teaspoon ground black pepper
- 1 1/2 teaspoons ground nutmeg
- 4 tablespoon olive oil

Method:

1. Pat dry chicken, then season with salt and black pepper on both sides and let it marinate for 30 minutes at room temperature.
2. Then switch on the air fryer, insert fryer basket, grease it with olive oil, then shut with its lid, set the fryer at 390 degrees F, and preheat for 5 minutes.
3. Meanwhile, brush chicken with oil and then season with remaining spices.
4. Open the fryer, add chicken thighs in it in a single layer, close with its lid and cook for 10 minutes until nicely golden and thoroughly cooked, shaking the basket every 5 minutes and turning the chicken halfway through.
5. When air fryer beeps, open its lid, transfer chicken onto a plate, wrap with aluminum foil to keep it warm, and cook the remaining chicken in the same manner.
6. Serve straight away.

Nutrition Value:

- Calories: 202 Cal
- Fat: 13.4 g
- Carbs: 1.7 g
- Protein: 25 g
- Fiber: 0.4 g

Cornish Hens

Servings: 4
Preparation time: 10 minutes
Cooking time: 1 hour and 30 minutes

Ingredients:

- 2 Cornish game hens
- ½ teaspoon dried thyme
- 1 teaspoon garlic powder
- ½ teaspoon dried oregano
- 1 tablespoon salt
- 1 teaspoon smoked paprika
- 1 teaspoon ground black pepper
- ½ teaspoon dried basil
- 2 tablespoons olive oil

Method:

1. Switch on the air fryer, insert fryer basket, grease it with non-stick cooking oil spray, then shut with its lid, set the fryer at 390 degrees F, and preheat for 5 minutes.
2. Meanwhile, take a small bowl, place oil in it, add all the seasonings, stir until combined and then rub this mixture all over the game hens until well coated.
3. Open the fryer, arrange a game hen in the air fryer basket, close with its lid and cook for 45 minutes until thoroughly cooked and golden brown, turning halfway.
4. Cook the remaining game hen in the same manner, cut into pieces and then serve.

Nutrition Value:

- Calories: 400 Cal
- Fat: 31 g
- Carbs: 1 g
- Protein: 29 g
- Fiber: 0.2 g

Tender Chicken Breasts

Preparation time: 10 minutes
Cooking time: 22 minutes
Servings: 4

Ingredients:

- 4 chicken breasts, each about 8 ounces, boneless, skinless
- ½ teaspoon garlic powder
- 1/8 teaspoon ground black pepper
- ½ teaspoon salt
- ½ teaspoon dried oregano
- 2 tablespoons olive oil

Method:

1. Switch on the air fryer, insert fryer basket, grease it with non-stick cooking oil spray, then shut with its lid, set the fryer at 360 degrees F, and preheat for 5 minutes.
2. Meanwhile, take a small bowl, place garlic powder, salt, black pepper and oregano and then stir until well combined.
3. Brush oil on both sides of the chicken and then season with the spice mix until coated.
4. Open the fryer, arrange the prepared chicken breasts in the air fryer basket in a single layer, close with its lid and cook for 20 to 22 minutes until thoroughly cooked and golden brown, turning halfway.
5. Serve straight away.

Nutrition Value:

- Calories: 163 Cal
- Fat: 3 g
- Carbs: 1 g
- Protein: 30 g
- Fiber: 0.4 g

Chapter 4: Appetizers and Siders

Zucchini Strips

Preparation time: 5 minutes
Cooking time: 14 minutes
Servings: 2

Ingredients:

- 2 large zucchini, ½-inch thick sliced lengthwise
- ½ teaspoon garlic powder
- 1/3 teaspoon salt
- ¼ teaspoon ground black pepper
- 2 tablespoons olive oil

Method:

1. Switch on the air fryer, insert fryer basket, grease it with non-stick cooking oil spray, then shut with its lid, set the fryer at 390 degrees F, and preheat for 5 minutes.
2. Meanwhile, brush the zucchini slices with oil and then season with garlic powder, salt and black pepper.
3. Open the fryer, arrange zucchini slices in the air fryer basket in a single layer, close with its lid and cook for 8 to 14 minutes until thoroughly cooked and golden brown, turning halfway.
4. Serve straight away.

Nutrition Value:

- Calories: 36 Cal
- Fat: 1 g
- Carbs: 7 g
- Protein: 2 g
- Fiber: 2 g

Quiche

Preparation time: 5 minutes
Cooking time: 10 minutes
Servings: 1

Ingredients:

- 4 florets of broccoli
- 1 tablespoon vegan cheddar cheese
- 4 tablespoons vegan heavy cream
- 1 egg

Method:

1. Switch on the air fryer, insert fryer basket, then shut with its lid, set the fryer at 325 degrees F, and preheat for 5 minutes.
2. Meanwhile, take a 5-inch heat-proof quiche dish, grease it with oil, crack the egg in it and then whisk in cream.
3. Scatter broccoli florets on top of the mixture and then sprinkle with cheese.
4. Open the fryer, place the quiche dish in the air fryer basket, close with its lid and cook for 10 minutes until thoroughly cooked, turning halfway.
5. Serve straight away.

Nutrition Value:

- Calories: 656 Cal
- Fat: 58 g
- Carbs: 18 g
- Protein: 21 g
- Fiber: 6 g

Zucchini Fritters

Preparation time: 15 minutes
Cooking time: 12 minutes
Servings: 4

Ingredients:

- 2 large zucchini, grated
- ¼ teaspoon onion powder
- 3 tablespoons coconut flour
- 1 teaspoon garlic powder
- 1 tablespoon salt
- ¼ teaspoon ground black pepper
- ¼ teaspoon paprika
- 1 egg

Method:

1. Take a large bowl, place grated zucchini in it, stir in salt and then let it rest for 10 minutes.
2. Drain the zucchini, wrap it in a cheesecloth and then twist well to remove excess water from it.
3. Transfer zucchini to a cleaned bowl, add remaining ingredients and then stir until combined.
4. Switch on the air fryer, insert fryer basket, line it with perforated baking paper, grease it with non-stick cooking oil spray, then shut with its lid, set the fryer at 360 degrees F, and preheat for 5 minutes.
5. Open the fryer, spoon the zucchini mixture in the air fryer basket in a single layer, spray oil on the food, close with its lid and cook for 12 minutes until thoroughly cooked and golden brown, turning halfway.
6. Serve straight away.

Nutrition Value:

- Calories: 57 Cal
- Fat: 1 g
- Carbs: 8 g
- Protein: 3 g
- Fiber: 1 g

Patatas Bravas

Preparation time: 25 minutes
Cooking time: 20 minutes
Servings: 4

Ingredients:

- 12 ounces red potato, cut into 1-inch chunks
- 1/2 teaspoon ground black pepper
- 1/2 teaspoon sea salt
- 1 teaspoon garlic powder
- 1/2 teaspoon cayenne pepper
- 1 tablespoon smoked paprika
- 1 tablespoon coconut oil
- ¼ teaspoon dried chives
- Garlic aioli for serving

Method:

1. Take a pot, place it half-full of water over medium heat, bring the water to boil, add potato pieces, and cook for 6 minutes.
2. Then drain the potatoes, pat them dry, cool for 15 minutes and add them into a large bowl.
3. Add garlic into the potatoes, season with 1/8 teaspoon each of salt and black pepper, drizzle with oil and toss until coated.
4. Switch on the air fryer, insert fryer basket, grease it with olive oil, then shut with its lid, set the fryer at 390 degrees F, and preheat for 5 minutes.
5. Open the fryer, add potatoes in it in a single layer, spray them with olive oil, close with its lid and cook for 15 minutes until nicely golden and crispy, shaking the basket halfway through.
6. When air fryer beeps, open its lid, transfer potatoes to a bowl, add remaining ingredients, toss until coated, and serve them with garlic aioli.

Nutrition Value:

- Calories: 97 Cal
- Fat: 4 g
- Carbs: 15 g
- Protein: 1 g
- Fiber: 1 g

Latkes

Preparation time: 10 minutes
Cooking time: 12 minutes
Servings: 20

Ingredients:

- 1 ½ pound rutabaga, shredded
- ½ of medium white onion, peeled, finely chopped
- 2 teaspoons salt
- ¼ cup oats
- ½ teaspoon ground black pepper
- 2 eggs

Method:

1. Switch on the air fryer, insert fryer basket, grease it with non-stick cooking oil spray, then shut with its lid, set the fryer at 375 degrees F, and preheat for 5 minutes.
2. Meanwhile, wrap shredded rutabaga and onion in a kitchen towel and then twist to remove liquid in it.
3. Take a large bowl, place rutabaga and onion in it, add remaining ingredients and then stir until combined.
4. Spoon the rutabaga mixture in the air fryer basket in a single layer, close with its lid and cook for 12 minutes until thoroughly cooked and golden brown, turning halfway.
5. Serve straight away.

Nutrition Value:

- Calories: 206 Cal
- Fat: 13 g
- Carbs: 19.2 g
- Protein: 3.5 g
- Fiber: 1.2 g

Jicama Fries

Preparation time: 5 minutes
Cooking time: 15 minutes
Servings: 1

Ingredients:

- 1 medium jicama, peeled, cut into matchsticks
- ½ teaspoon garlic powder
- ¾ teaspoon salt
- 1 teaspoon paprika
- ½ teaspoon ground black pepper
- 2 tablespoons olive oil

Method:

1. Switch on the air fryer, insert fryer basket, grease it with non-stick cooking oil spray, then shut with its lid, set the fryer at 400 degrees F, and preheat for 5 minutes.
2. Meanwhile, take a large bowl, place jicama pieces in it, add remaining ingredients and then toss until combined.
3. Open the fryer, arrange jicama pieces in the air fryer basket in a single layer, close with its lid and cook for 15 minutes until thoroughly cooked, tossing every 5 minutes.
4. Serve straight away.

Nutrition Value:

- Calories: 125 Cal
- Fat: 7 g
- Carbs: 15 g
- Protein: 1 g
- Fiber: 8 g

Cauliflower

Preparation time: 5 minutes
Cooking time: 20 minutes
Servings: 5

Ingredients:

- 16 ounces cauliflower, cut into florets
- 2/3 teaspoon salt
- ½ teaspoon ground black pepper
- 2 teaspoons olive oil
- 1 tablespoon potato starch

Method:

1. Switch on the air fryer, insert fryer basket, grease it with olive oil, then shut with its lid, set the fryer at 400 degrees F, and preheat for 5 minutes.
2. Meanwhile, place cauliflower florets in a bowl, add remaining ingredients and toss until well coated.
3. Open the fryer, add cauliflower florets in it, close with its lid and cook for 15 minutes until nicely golden and crispy, shaking the basket every 5 minutes.
4. When air fryer beeps, open its lid, transfer cauliflower florets onto a serving plate and serve.

Nutrition Value:

- Calories: 36 Cal
- Fat: 1 g
- Carbs: 5 g
- Protein: 1 g
- Fiber: 1 g

Zucchini, Yellow Squash, and Carrots

Preparation time: 10 minutes
Cooking time: 40 minutes
Servings: 4

Ingredients:

- 1 pound zucchini, ends trimmed, cut into ¾-inch half moons
- ½ pound carrots, peeled, 1-inch cubed
- 1 pound yellow squash, ends trimmed, cut into ¾-inch half moons
- 1 tablespoon chopped tarragon
- ½ teaspoon ground white pepper
- 1 teaspoon salt
- 6 teaspoons olive oil

Method:

1. Switch on the air fryer, insert fryer basket, grease it with olive oil, then shut with its lid, set the fryer at 400 degrees F, and preheat for 5 minutes.
2. Meanwhile, place carrots in a bowl, drizzle with 2 teaspoon oil, and toss until combined.
3. Open the fryer, add carrot pieces in it, close with its lid and cook for 5 minutes until nicely golden and crispy, shaking the basket halfway through.
4. Meanwhile, place zucchini and squash pieces in a bowl, add remaining ingredients except for tarragon and toss until mixed.
5. When air fryer beeps, open the lid, add zucchini and squash into fryer basket, shut with its lid and cook for 30 minutes until nicely golden and crispy, shaking the basket every 10 minutes.
6. When done, transfer vegetables into a bowl, top with tarragon leaves and serve.

Nutrition Value:

- Calories: 121.5 Cal
- Fat: 7.4 g
- Carbs: 11.5 g
- Protein: 2.1 g
- Fiber: 4 g

Cauliflower Fritters

Preparation time: 10 minutes
Cooking time: 25 minutes
Servings: 4

Ingredients:

- ¼ of large cauliflower florets, chopped
- ½ cup coconut flour
- 1 ½ tablespoon chopped mint
- ½ cup buttermilk
- 3.5 ounces crumbled feta cheese
- 1 egg
- 3 tablespoons olive oil

Method:

1. Switch on the air fryer, insert fryer basket, grease it with non-stick cooking oil spray, then shut with its lid, set the fryer at 400 degrees F, and preheat for 5 minutes.
2. Meanwhile, take a large bowl, place cauliflower florets, add salt, black pepper and 1 ½ tablespoon and then toss until coated.
3. Open the fryer, place the cauliflower florets in the air fryer basket, close with its lid and cook for 15 minutes until thoroughly cooked, turning halfway.
4. Take a large bowl, crack the egg in it, whisk in flour and then whisk in milk until thick batter comes together.
5. Add cheese and mint, add cooked cauliflower and remaining oil and then stir until well combined.
6. Spoon the cauliflower mixture in the air fryer basket in a single layer, close with its lid and cook for 10 minutes until thoroughly cooked and golden brown, turning halfway.
7. Serve straight away.

Nutrition Value:

- Calories: 263 Cal
- Fat: 18 g
- Carbs: 17 g
- Protein: 9 g
- Fiber: 2 g

Mac and Cheese

Preparation time: 10 minutes
Cooking time: 30 minutes
Servings: 2

Ingredients:

- 1 cup elbow macaroni, whole-wheat
- 1/2 cup broccoli florets
- ¼ teaspoon ground black pepper
- 1/3 teaspoon salt
- 1 1/2 cup grated cheddar cheese
- 1 tablespoon grated parmesan cheese
- 1/2 cup almond milk, warmed

Method:

1. Take a pot half full of water, place it over medium-high heat, bring it to boil, then add macaroni and broccoli and cook for 10 minutes until tender.
2. When done, drain macaroni and vegetables, transfer them in a bowl, pour in milk, add cheddar cheese, season with black pepper and salt, and stir until well mixed.
3. Switch on the air fryer, insert fryer basket, then shut with its lid, set the fryer at 350 degrees F, and preheat for 5 minutes.
4. Meanwhile, place mac and cheese mixture in a heatproof baking dish that fits into the air fryer and sprinkle parmesan cheese on top.
5. Open the fryer, place baking dish in it, close with its lid and cook for 15 minutes until pasta is bubbling.
6. When air fryer beeps, open its lid, take out the baking dish, let the pasta sit for 10 minutes, and then serve.

Nutrition Value:

- Calories: 320 Cal
- Fat: 17 g
- Carbs: 29 g
- Protein: 15 g
- Fiber: 2.8 g

Spiced Okra Fries

Preparation time: 5 minutes
Cooking time: 15 minutes
Servings: 4

Ingredients:

- 15 ounces okra, fresh
- ½ teaspoon garlic powder
- 1 teaspoon paprika
- 1 teaspoon red chili powder
- 2 tablespoons olive oil

Method:

1. Switch on the air fryer, insert fryer basket, grease it with non-stick cooking oil spray, then shut with its lid, set the fryer at 400 degrees F, and preheat for 5 minutes.
2. Meanwhile, take a large bowl, place okra in it, add remaining ingredients and then toss until coated.
3. Open the fryer, arrange okra in the air fryer basket in a single layer, close with its lid and cook for 15 minutes until thoroughly cooked, turning halfway.
4. Serve straight away.

Nutrition Value:

- Calories: 100 Cal
- Fat: 7 g
- Carbs: 9 g
- Protein: 2 g
- Fiber: 4 g

Seasoned Rutabaga Fries

Preparation time: 5 minutes
Cooking time: 15 minutes
Servings: 4

Ingredients:

- 1 rutabaga, peeled, cut into 1/2-inch wedges
- ¼ teaspoon garlic powder
- ½ teaspoon onion powder
- ½ teaspoon salt
- 1 teaspoon paprika
- ¼ teaspoon ground black pepper
- ½ teaspoon dried parsley
- 1 tablespoon olive oil

Method:

1. Switch on the air fryer, insert fryer basket, grease it with non-stick cooking oil spray, then shut with its lid, set the fryer at 400 degrees F, and preheat for 5 minutes.
2. Meanwhile, take a large bowl, place rutabaga wedges in it, add remaining ingredients and then toss until coated.
3. Open the fryer, arrange rutabaga wedges in the air fryer basket in a single layer, close with its lid and cook for 15 minutes until thoroughly cooked and golden brown, turning halfway.
4. Serve straight away.

Nutrition Value:

- Calories: 70 Cal
- Fat: 4 g
- Carbs: 9 g
- Protein: 1 g
- Fiber: 2 g

Sweet Potato Cauliflower Patties

Preparation time: 15 minutes
Cooking time: 52 minutes
Servings: 10

Ingredients:

- 1 large sweet potato, peeled, diced
- 2 cup cauliflower florets
- 1 green onion, chopped
- 1 cup cilantro
- 1 teaspoon minced garlic
- 1/4 teaspoon salt
- 1/4 teaspoon ground black pepper
- 2 tablespoons ranch seasoning mix
- 2 tablespoons arrowroot starch
- 1/2 teaspoon red chili powder
- 1/4 cup ground flaxseed
- 1/4 teaspoon cumin
- 1/4 cup sunflower seeds

Method:

1. Place sweet potato pieces in a food processor and pulse until coarsely chopped.
2. Then add cauliflower florets along with garlic and onion and pulse again until combined.
3. Add remaining, pulse for 1 minute until thick batter comes together, then shape the batter into 8 to 10 patties and freeze them for 10 minutes.
4. Switch on the air fryer, insert fryer basket, grease it with olive oil, then shut with its lid, set the fryer at 370 degrees F, and preheat for 5 minutes.
5. Open the fryer, add prepared patties in it in a single layer, spray them with oil, close with its lid, and cook for 18 minutes until nicely golden and crispy, turning the patties halfway through.
6. When air fryer beeps, open its lid, transfer patties onto a serving plate, keep them warm and cook remaining patties in the same manner.
7. Serve straight away.

Nutrition Value:

- Calories: 85 Cal
- Fat: 3 g
- Carbs: 9 g
- Protein: 2.7 g
- Fiber: 3.5 g

Whole-Wheat Pizzas

Preparation time: 10 minutes
Cooking time: 25 minutes
Servings: 2

Ingredients:

- 2 whole-wheat pita rounds
- 1 small tomato, cut into eight slices
- ½ teaspoon minced garlic
- 1 cup baby spinach leaves
- 1/4 cup marinara sauce
- 1/4 cup shredded mozzarella cheese
- 1 tablespoon grated parmesan cheese

Method:

1. Switch on the air fryer, insert fryer basket, grease it with olive oil, then shut with its lid, set the fryer at 350 degrees F, and preheat for 10 minutes.
2. Meanwhile, prepare pizzas and for this, spread 1 tablespoon of marinara sauce on one side of each pita bread, then evenly top with spinach and tomatoes, and then sprinkle with garlic and cheeses.
3. Open the fryer, add one pizza in it, close with its lid and cook for 5 minutes until nicely golden and crispy.
4. When air fryer beeps, open its lid, transfer the pizza onto a serving plate, keep it warm, and cook remaining pizza in the same manner.
5. Serve straight away.

Nutrition Value:

- Calories: 229 Cal
- Fat: 5 g
- Carbs: 37 g
- Protein: 11 g
- Fiber: 5 g

Cauliflower Rice

Preparation time: 10 minutes
Cooking time: 27 minutes
Servings: 3

Ingredients:

- 6 ounces tofu, pressed, drained
- 1/2 cup diced white onion
- 1/2 cup frozen peas
- 3 cups riced cauliflower
- 1/2 cup chopped broccoli florets
- 1 cup diced carrot
- 1 tablespoon minced ginger
- 1 teaspoon minced garlic
- 1 teaspoon turmeric powder
- 1 tablespoon apple cider vinegar
- 4 tablespoons soy sauce
- 1 1/2 teaspoons toasted sesame oil

Method:

1. Switch on the air fryer, insert fryer baking pan, grease it with olive oil, then shut with its lid, set the fryer at 370 degrees F, and preheat for 5 minutes.
2. Meanwhile, place them in a large bowl, crumble it, add onion, carrot, sprinkle with turmeric, drizzle with 2 tablespoons soy sauce and toss until mixed.
3. Open the fryer, add tofu in it, spray with olive oil, close with its lid and cook for 10 minutes until nicely golden, shaking the basket halfway through.
4. Meanwhile, place remaining ingredients in a bowl, toss until well mixed and set aside until required.
5. When air fryer beeps, open its lid, add remaining ingredients into the tofu, shake gently until just mixed, close with its lid, and cook for 12 minutes until nicely golden and cooked through, shaking the basket halfway through.
6. Serve straight away.

Nutrition Value:

- Calories: 153 Cal
- Fat: 4 g
- Carbs: 18 g
- Protein: 9 g
- Fiber: 6 g

Turnip Fries

Preparation time: 5 minutes
Cooking time: 20 minutes
Servings: 4

Ingredients:

- 2 pounds turnips, peeled, cut to ½-inch sticks
- 2 tablespoons cornstarch
- ½ teaspoon onion powder
- 1 teaspoon garlic powder
- ½ teaspoon salt
- ¼ teaspoon ground black pepper
- 1 teaspoon paprika
- 2 tablespoons olive oil

Method:

1. Switch on the air fryer, insert fryer basket, grease it with non-stick cooking oil spray, then shut with its lid, set the fryer at 400 degrees F, and preheat for 5 minutes.
2. Meanwhile, take a large bowl, place turnips in it, sprinkle with cornstarch and then toss until coated.
3. Take a small bowl, add salt, black pepper, onion powder, garlic powder, paprika and oil and then stir until combined.
4. Drizzle this mixture over the turnips and then toss until coated.
5. Open the fryer, arrange turnip sticks in the air fryer basket in a single layer, close with its lid and cook for 20 minutes until thoroughly cooked and crispy, turning halfway.
6. Serve straight away.

Nutrition Value:

- Calories: 115 Cal
- Fat: 4.3 g
- Carbs: 18.2 g
- Protein: 0.8 g
- Fiber: 4.8 g

Chicken Nuggets

Preparation time: 10 minutes
Cooking time: 35 minutes
Servings: 6

Ingredients:

- 1 cup almond flour
- 2 pounds of chicken breast
- 1/2 teaspoon garlic powder
- 1 teaspoon onion flakes
- 1/2 teaspoon salt
- 4 tablespoons olive oil
- 1 egg, beaten

Method:

1. Take a shallow dish, add flour in it, season with onion powder, salt, and garlic and stir well.
2. Crack the egg in a bowl, add oil, and whisk well until incorporated.
3. Cut chicken breast into bite-size pieces, then dredge with almond flour mixture and coat with egg mixture.
4. Switch on the air fryer, insert fryer basket, grease it with olive oil, then shut with its lid, set the fryer at 350 degrees F, and preheat for 5 minutes.
5. Open the fryer, add chicken nuggets in it in a single layer, close with its lid and cook for 15 minutes until nicely golden and crispy, shaking the basket every 5 minutes and turning chicken nuggets halfway through.
6. When air fryer beeps, open its lid, transfer chicken nuggets onto a serving plate, keep them warm and cook remaining chicken nuggets in the same manner.
7. Serve straight away.

Nutrition Value:

- Calories: 445 Cal
- Fat: 25.5 g
- Carbs: 4.5 g
- Protein: 48.8 g
- Fiber: 2 g

Chapter 5: Beef, Pork, and Lamb

Garlic Butter Pork Chops

Preparation time: 10 minutes
Cooking time: 30 minutes
Servings: 2

Ingredients:

- 4 pork chops, each about 6 ounces
- 2 teaspoons minced garlic
- 1 teaspoon salt
- 1 teaspoon ground black pepper
- 2 teaspoons chopped parsley
- 1 tablespoon coconut butter
- 1 tablespoon coconut oil

Method:

1. Take a small bowl, place garlic, butter and coconut oil, add all the seasonings and then stir until mixed.
2. Rub the spice mix on both sides of pork chops, seal them in aluminum foil and then let them marinate for a minimum of 1 hour in the refrigerator.
3. When ready to cook, switch on the air fryer, insert the fryer basket, grease it with non-stick cooking oil spray, then shut with its lid, set the fryer at 350 degrees F, and preheat for 5 minutes.
4. Meanwhile, remove pork chops from the refrigerator and uncover them.
5. Open the fryer, arrange the pork chops in the air fryer basket in a single layer, close with its lid and cook for 15 minutes until thoroughly cooked and golden brown, turning halfway.
6. Serve straight away.

Nutrition Value:

- Calories: 524 Cal
- Fat: 29 g
- Carbs: 2 g
- Protein: 58 g
- Fiber: 1 g

Southern Style Pork Chops

Preparation time: 10 minutes
Cooking time: 15 minutes
Servings: 4

Ingredients:

- 4 pork chops, boneless
- ½ teaspoon salt
- ¼ cup almond flour
- ½ teaspoon ground black pepper
- 3 tablespoons buttermilk

Method:

1. Prepare the pork chops and for this, season them with salt and black pepper and then drizzle with milk.
2. Take a large plastic bag
3. place flour in it and then add seasoned pork chops.
4. Seal the bag
5. turn it upside down until pork chops are coated in flour and then let them marinate for 30 minutes.
6. When ready to cook, switch on the air fryer, insert the fryer basket, grease it with non-stick cooking oil spray, then shut with its lid, set the fryer at 380 degrees F, and preheat for 5 minutes.
7. Open the fryer, arrange the pork chops in the air fryer basket in a single layer, spray oil on the food, close with its lid and cook for 15 minutes until thoroughly cooked and golden brown, turning halfway.
8. Serve straight away.

Nutrition Value:

- Calories: 296 Cal
- Fat: 13.4 g
- Carbs: 23.4 g
- Protein: 20 g
- Fiber: 0.3 g

Beef and Mushroom Patties

Preparation time: 10 minutes
Cooking time: 20 minutes
Servings: 5

Ingredients:

- 1 pound ground beef
- 6 medium mushrooms
- 1 teaspoon onion powder
- 1/2 teaspoon salt
- 1 teaspoon garlic powder
- 1/2 teaspoon ground black pepper
- 1 tablespoon Maggi seasoning sauce

Method:

1. Switch on the air fryer, insert fryer basket, grease it with olive oil, then shut with its lid, set the fryer at 320 degrees F, and preheat for 10 minutes.
2. Meanwhile, rinse mushrooms, drain them well, add them in a food processor and then pulse until puree.
3. Then add remaining ingredients except for ground beef and pulse for 1 minute until smooth.
4. Tip the mushroom mixture in a bowl, add turkey, stir well and then shape the mixture into five patties.
5. Open the fryer, add patties in it in a single layer, spray with olive oil, close with its lid and cook for 10 minutes until nicely golden and cook through, shaking the basket every 5 minutes and flipping the patties halfway through.
6. When air fryer beeps, open its lid, transfer patties onto a serving plate, and serve.

Nutrition Value:

- Calories: 221.4 Cal
- Fat: 8.3 g
- Carbs: 11.1 g
- Protein: 26.4 g
- Fiber: 2.5 g

Glazed Pork Tenderloin

Preparation time: 10 minutes
Cooking time: 20 minutes
Servings: 4

Ingredients:

- 1.5-pound pork tenderloin, fat trimmed
- 2 cloves of garlic, peeled, sliced
- 1 teaspoon dried rosemary
- ¼ teaspoon salt
- 3 tablespoons coconut sugar
- ⅛ teaspoon ground black pepper
- 1 teaspoon Italian seasoning
- ¼ cup yellow mustard

Method:

1. Prepare the pork tenderloin and for this, make some slits in it and then stuff with garlic.
2. Take a small bowl, place all the seasonings and mustard in it and then stir until combined.
3. Rub the prepared spice mix all over the pork and then let it marinate for a minimum of 2 hours in the refrigerator.
4. When ready to cook, switch on the air fryer, insert the fryer basket, grease it with non-stick cooking oil spray, then shut with its lid, set the fryer at 400 degrees F, and preheat for 5 minutes.
5. Open the fryer, arrange the marinated pork tenderloin in the air fryer basket, spray oil on the food, close with its lid and cook for 20 minutes until thoroughly cooked, turning halfway.
6. When done, let the pork tenderloin rest for 5 minutes, cut it into slices and then serve.

Nutrition Value:

- Calories: 390 Cal
- Fat: 11 g
- Carbs: 11 g
- Protein: 59 g
- Fiber: 1 g

Crispy Pork Chops

Preparation time: 10 minutes
Cooking time: 12 minutes
Servings: 6

Ingredients:

- 1 ½ pound pork chops, boneless
- 1/3 cup oats
- 1 teaspoon garlic powder
- 1 teaspoon paprika
- 1 teaspoon creole seasoning
- ¼ cup vegan grated parmesan cheese

Method:

1. Switch on the air fryer, insert fryer basket, grease it with non-stick cooking oil spray, then shut with its lid, set the fryer at 360 degrees F, and preheat for 5 minutes.
2. Meanwhile, take a large plastic bag and place all the ingredients in it.
3. Seal the bag and then turn it upside down until pork chops are coated with the oat mixture.
4. Open the fryer, arrange pork chops in the air fryer basket in a single layer, spray oil on the food, close with its lid and cook for 12 minutes until thoroughly cooked and golden brown, turning halfway.
5. Serve straight away.

Nutrition Value:

- Calories: 231 Cal
- Fat: 12 g
- Carbs: 2 g
- Protein: 27 g
- Fiber: 1 g

Meatloaf Sliders

Preparation time: 10 minutes
Cooking time: 30 minutes
Servings: 8

Ingredients:

- 1 pound ground beef
- ½ cup almond flour
- ¼ cup chopped red onion
- ¼ cup coconut flour
- 1 teaspoon minced garlic
- 1 teaspoon Italian seasoning
- ½ teaspoon ground black pepper
- ½ teaspoon of sea salt
- 1 tablespoon Worcestershire sauce
- ½ teaspoon dried tarragon
- 2 eggs, beaten
- ¼ cup ketchup

Method:

1. Place all the ingredients in a large bowl and mix well until combined.
2. Then shape the mixture into eight patties and refrigerate them for 10 minutes until firm.
3. Then switch on the air fryer, insert fryer basket, grease it with olive oil, then shut with its lid, set the fryer at 360 degrees F, and preheat for 10 minutes.
4. Open the fryer, add meatloaf slider in it in a single layer, spray with oil, close with its lid and cook for 10 minutes until nicely golden and thoroughly cooked, shaking the basket every 5 minutes and turning the sliders halfway through.
5. When air fryer beeps, open its lid, transfer sliders onto a serving plate, keep them warm and cook remaining sliders in the same manner.
6. Serve straight away.

Nutrition Value:

- Calories: 228 Cal
- Fat: 17 g
- Carbs: 6 g
- Protein: 13 g
- Fiber: 2 g

Pork Dumplings with Dipping Sauce

Preparation time: 10 minutes
Cooking time: 52 minutes
Servings: 4

Ingredients:

- 4 ounces ground pork
- 4 cups chopped bok choy
- 1 teaspoon olive oil
- 1 tablespoon grated ginger
- 1 tablespoon minced garlic
- 1/4 teaspoon crushed red pepper
- 18 dumpling wrappers, about 3 1/2-inch square

For the Dip:

- 1 tablespoon chopped scallions
- 1/2 teaspoon coconut sugar
- 2 tablespoons apple cider vinegar
- 2 teaspoons soy sauce
- 1 teaspoon toasted sesame oil

Method:

1. Take a skillet pan, place it over medium-high heat, add oil and when hot, add bok choy, stir and cook for 6 to 8 minutes until wilted.
2. Then stir in garlic and ginger, cook for 1 minute until fragrant, then remove the pan from heat, let bok choy cool for 5 minutes and then pat dry with paper towels.
3. Spoon bok choy mixture in a bowl, add ground pork and crushed red pepper and stir until well combined.
4. Prepare the dumplings and for this, place a dumpling wrapper on clean working space, place 1 tablespoon of pork mixture in the center, then brush water on the edges, and then fold it over the filling to make half-moon shape dumpling.
5. Press the edges of wrap to seal the dumplings, place it on a plate, and prepare remaining dumplings in the same manner.
6. Switch on the air fryer, insert fryer basket, grease it with olive oil, then shut with its lid, set the fryer at 375 degrees F, and preheat for 5 minutes.
7. Open the fryer, add dumplings in it in a single layer, spray with oil, close with its lid and cook for 12 minutes until nicely golden brown and cooked, shaking the basket every 5 minutes and turning the dumpling halfway.
8. In the meantime, prepare the dip and for this, place all its ingredients in a bowl and whisk until combined.

9. When air fryer beeps, open its lid, transfer dumplings onto a serving plate, keep warm and cook remaining dumplings in the same manner.

Nutrition Value:

- Calories: 140 Cal
- Fat: 5 g
- Carbs: 16 g
- Protein: 7 g
- Fiber: 1 g

Herbed Lamb Chops

Preparation time: 5 minutes
Cooking time: 22 minutes
Servings: 4

Ingredients:

- 1 pound lamb chops
- 1 teaspoon salt
- 1 teaspoon dried oregano
- 1 teaspoon dried rosemary
- 1 teaspoon coriander
- 1 teaspoon dried thyme
- 2 tablespoons lemon juice
- 2 tablespoons olive oil

Method:

1. Place all the ingredients except for lamb in a large plastic bag, seal the bag, and shake until well mixed.
2. Add lamb chops into the plastic bag, seal the bag, shake until well coated and marinate in the refrigerator for a minimum of 1 hour.
3. Then switch on the air fryer, insert fryer basket, grease it with olive oil, then shut with its lid, set the fryer at 390 degrees F, and preheat for 5 minutes.
4. Then open the fryer, add lamb chops in it in a single layer, spray with olive oil, close with its lid and cook for 8 minutes until nicely golden and cooked through, shaking the basket every 5 minutes, flipping lamb chops halfway through.
5. When air fryer beeps, open its lid, transfer lamb chops onto a serving plate, keep them warm and cook remaining lamb chops in the same manner.
6. Serve straight away.

Nutrition Value:

- Calories: 280 Cal
- Fat: 12.3 g
- Carbs: 8.3 g
- Protein: 32.7 g
- Fiber: 1.2 g

Steak Nuggets

Preparation time: 40 minutes
Cooking time: 15 minutes
Servings: 4

Ingredients:

- 1 pound beef steak, cut into chunks
- 1 large egg

For Breading:

- 1/2 teaspoon seasoned salt
- 1/2 cup pork panko
- 1/2 cup grated parmesan cheese

For Chipotle Ranch Dip:

- 1/4 of a medium lime, juiced
- 1/2 teaspoon ranch dressing and dip mix
- 1 teaspoon chipotle paste
- 1/4 cup mayonnaise
- 1/4 cup sour cream

Method:

1. Prepare the ranch dip and for this, place all its ingredients in a bowl and whisk well until mixed; reserve its 1 teaspoon and refrigerate until required.
2. Prepare breading and for this, place all its ingredients in a shallow dish and stir until mixed.
3. Crack the egg in a bowl and then whisk well until blended.
4. Prepare nuggets and for this, dip steak pieces into the egg, then dredge into the breading until coated, arrange them on a sheet pan lined with baking paper and freeze for 30 minutes.
5. Then switch on the air fryer, insert fryer basket, grease it with olive oil, then shut with its lid, set the fryer at 325 degrees F, and preheat for 5 minutes.
6. Open the fryer, add steak nuggets in it in a single layer, spray with olive oil, close with its lid and cook for 3 minutes until nicely golden and cooked.
7. When air fryer beeps, open its lid, transfer nuggets onto a serving plate, keep warm and cook remaining nuggets in the same manner.
8. Serve nuggets with ranch dip.

Nutrition Value:

- Calories: 350 Cal
- Fat: 20 g
- Carbs: 1 g
- Protein: 40 g
- Fiber: 0 g

Italian-Style Meatballs

Preparation time: 15 minutes
Cooking time: 25 minutes
Servings: 4

Ingredients:

- 2/3 pound ground beef
- 2 tablespoons minced shallots
- 1/3 pound turkey sausage
- 1 tablespoon minced garlic
- 1/4 cup chopped parsley
- 1 tablespoon Dijon mustard
- 1/2 teaspoon salt
- 1 tablespoon chopped thyme
- 1 tablespoon chopped rosemary
- 2 tablespoons olive oil
- 1 egg, beaten
- 1/4 cup whole-wheat panko crumbs
- 2 tablespoons almond milk
- Zucchini noodles for serving

Method:

1. Place panko crumbs in a bowl, add milk, stir and let it stand for 5 minutes.
2. Meanwhile, take a skillet pan, place it over medium-high heat, add oil and when hot, add shallots and cook for 2 minutes until softened.
3. Then add minced garlic, cook for 1 minute until fragrant, and then remove the pan from heat.
4. Add shallot mixture in a large bowl, pour in milk mixture along with sausage, beef, salt, thyme, rosemary, mustard, and parsley and stir until combined.
5. Switch on the air fryer, insert fryer basket, grease it with olive oil, then shut with its lid, set the fryer at 400 degrees F, and preheat for 5 minutes.
6. Meanwhile, prepare meatballs and for this, shape the beef mixture into 1 ½ inch meatballs.
7. Open the fryer, add meatballs in it in a single layer, spray them with olive oil, close with its lid and cook for 10 minutes until nicely golden and cooked through, shaking the basket every 5 minutes and turning meatballs halfway through.
8. When air fryer beeps, open its lid, transfer meatballs onto a serving plate, keep them warm and cook remaining meatballs in the same manner.
9. Serve meatballs with zucchini noodles.

Nutrition Value:

- Calories: 122 Cal
- Fat: 8 g
- Carbs: 0 g
- Protein: 10 g
- Fiber: 0 g

Rib Eye Steak

Preparation time: 10 minutes
Cooking time: 17 minutes
Servings: 1

Ingredients:

- 16 ounces rib-eye steak, about 1 ½-inch thick
- 1/2 teaspoon garlic powder
- 1 teaspoon salt
- 3/4 teaspoon ground black pepper
- 3/4 teaspoon steak seasoning

Method:

1. Switch on the air fryer, insert fryer basket, grease it with olive oil, then shut with its lid, set the fryer at 350 degrees F, and preheat for 5 minutes.
2. Meanwhile, stir together garlic powder, salt, black pepper, and steak seasoning and then sprinkle it on all sides of steak.
3. Open the fryer, add steak in it, spray with olive oil, close with its lid, and cook for 12 minutes until nicely golden and thoroughly cooked, turning and spraying with olive oil halfway through.
4. When air fryer beeps, open its lid, transfer steak onto a serving plate, cover it with foil, and let it rest for 10 minutes, then cut it into slices and serve.

Nutrition Value:

- Calories: 230 Cal
- Fat: 16 g
- Carbs: 0 g
- Protein: 21 g
- Fiber: 0 g

Pork Chops

Preparation time: 10 minutes
Cooking time: 28 minutes
Servings: 4

Ingredients:

- 4 pork chops, bone-in
- 1 teaspoon onion powder
- 1 teaspoon garlic powder
- 1/8 teaspoon allspice
- 1 teaspoon dried parsley
- 1 teaspoon paprika
- 2 cups crushed pork rinds

Method:

1. Switch on the air fryer, insert fryer basket, grease it with olive oil, then shut with its lid, set the fryer at 400 degrees F, and preheat for 10 minutes.
2. Meanwhile, prepare pork chops, and for this, brush them with olive oil on both sides until coated.
3. Place the remaining ingredients in a small bowl and then dredge pork chops in it until evenly coated.
4. Open the fryer, add pork chops in it, close with its lid and cook for 18 minutes until nicely golden and crispy, shaking the basket every 5 minutes, flipping the pork chops halfway through.
5. When air fryer beeps, open its lid, transfer pork chops onto a serving plate and serve.

Nutrition Value:

- Calories: 371 Cal
- Fat: 20 g
- Carbs: 1 g
- Protein: 44 g
- Fiber: 1 g

Spicy Bacon Bites

Preparation time: 5 minutes
Cooking time: 15 minutes
Servings: 2

Ingredients:

- 4 strips of bacon
- 1/2 cup crushed pork rinds
- 1/4 cup hot sauce

Method:

1. Switch on the air fryer, insert fryer basket, grease it with olive oil, then shut with its lid, set the fryer at 350 degrees F, and preheat for 5 minutes.
2. Meanwhile, cut bacon into six pieces, place them in a bowl, drizzle with hot sauce, then toss until coated and dredge with pork rinds.
3. Open the fryer, add bacon pieces in it, spray with olive oil, close with its lid and cook for 10 minutes until nicely golden and crispy, shaking the basket every 5 minutes.
4. When air fryer beeps, open its lid, transfer bacon onto a serving plate and serve.

Nutrition Value:

- Calories: 120.7 Cal
- Fat: 8.7 g
- Carbs: 0 g
- Protein: 7.3 g
- Fiber: 0 g

Pork Chops with Brussels Sprouts

Preparation time: 5 minutes
Cooking time: 30 minutes
Servings: 1

Ingredients:

- 1 pork chop, bone-in, center-cut, about 8 ounces
- 6 ounces Brussels sprouts, cut into quarters
- 1/8 teaspoon salt
- 1 teaspoon agave syrup
- ½ teaspoon ground black pepper, divided
- 1 teaspoon mustard paste
- 1 teaspoon olive oil

Method:

1. Switch on the air fryer, insert fryer basket, grease it with non-stick cooking oil spray, then shut with its lid, set the fryer at 400 degrees F, and preheat for 5 minutes.
2. Meanwhile, rub the pork chop with oil and then season with salt and ¼ teaspoon black pepper.
3. Take a medium bowl, place remaining ingredients in it, add Brussels sprouts and then toss until coated.
4. Open the fryer, arrange pork chops and Brussels sprouts in the air fryer basket, close with its lid and cook for 13 minutes until thoroughly cooked and golden brown, turning halfway.
5. Serve straight away.

Nutrition Value:

- Calories: 337 Cal
- Fat: 11 g
- Carbs: 21 g
- Protein: 40 g
- Fiber: 10 g

Spicy Lamb Steak

Preparation time: 40 minutes
Cooking time: 35 minutes
Servings: 4

Ingredients:

- 1 pound lamb sirloin steaks, boneless
- 4 slices of ginger
- 1/2 of a white onion
- 5 cloves of garlic, peeled
- 1 teaspoon ground fennel
- 1 teaspoon salt
- 1/2 teaspoon ground cardamom
- 1 teaspoon cayenne pepper
- 1 teaspoon garam masala
- 1 teaspoon ground cinnamon

Method:

1. Place all the ingredients in a blender, except for lamb, and pulse for 4 minutes until blended.
2. Place lamb chops in a bowl, make cuts in it with a knife, add marinade, toss until well coated and marinate for a minimum for 30 minutes.
3. Then switch on the air fryer, insert fryer basket, grease it with olive oil, then shut with its lid, set the fryer at 330 degrees F, and preheat for 5 minutes.
4. Open the fryer, add lamb steaks in it in a single layer, spray them with oil, close with its lid and cook for 15 minutes until nicely golden and cooked through, shaking the basket every 5 minutes, flipping halfway through.
5. When air fryer beeps, open its lid, transfer lamb steaks onto a serving plate, keep it warm and cook remaining steaks in the same manner.
6. Serve straight away.

Nutrition Value:

- Calories: 182 Cal
- Fat: 7 g
- Carbs: 3 g
- Protein: 24 g
- Fiber: 1 g

Chapter 6: Vegetarian

Roasted Rainbow Vegetables

Preparation time: 5 minutes
Cooking time: 25 minutes
Servings: 4

Ingredients:

- 1 medium red bell pepper, deseeded, 1-inch cubed
- 4 ounces mushrooms, halved
- 1 medium yellow summer squash, deseeded, 1-inch cubed
- 1/2 of sweet onion, peeled, cut into 1-inch wedges
- 1 medium zucchini, 1-inch cubed
- ½ teaspoon salt
- ½ teaspoon ground black pepper
- 1 tablespoon olive oil

Method:

1. Switch on the air fryer, insert fryer basket, grease it with olive oil, then shut with its lid, set the fryer at 350 degrees F, and preheat for 5 minutes.
2. Meanwhile, place all the ingredients in a large bowl and toss until well coated.
3. Open the fryer, add vegetables in it in an even layer, close with its lid and cook for 20 minutes until nicely golden and crispy, shaking the basket every 5 minutes, stirring halfway through.
4. When air fryer beeps, open its lid, transfer vegetables onto a serving plate and serve.

Nutrition Value:

- Calories: 69 Cal
- Fat: 3.8 g
- Carbs: 7.7 g
- Protein: 2.6 g
- Fiber: 2.3 g

Green Beans with Bacon

Preparation time: 5 minutes
Cooking time: 25 minutes
Servings: 4

Ingredients:

- 3 slices of bacon, diced
- 1 teaspoon ground black pepper
- 3 cups cut green beans
- 1 teaspoon salt
- 1/4 cup water

Method:

1. Switch on the air fryer, insert fryer basket, then shut with its lid, set the fryer at 375 degrees F, and preheat for 5 minutes.
2. Meanwhile, take a baking pan that fits into the air fryer, add bacon, onion, and green beans in it, pour in water, and stir until just mixed.
3. Then open the fryer, add baking pan in it, close with its lid, cook for 15 minutes, stirring the beans halfway through.
4. Then season beans and bacon with salt, stir well, set the fryer temperature to 400 degrees F, and continue cooking for 5 minutes.
5. When air fryer beeps, open its lid, take out the pan, cover it, and then let green beans and bacon rest for 5 minutes.
6. Serve straight away.

Nutrition Value:

- Calories: 95 Cal
- Fat: 6 g
- Carbs: 6 g
- Protein: 3 g
- Fiber: 2 g

Yellow Squash

Preparation time: 5 minutes
Cooking time: 10 minutes
Servings: 4

Ingredients:

- 2 medium yellow squash, peeled, cored, ¾-inch sliced
- ¼ teaspoon salt
- 1/8 teaspoon ground black pepper
- 2 teaspoons olive oil

Method:

1. Switch on the air fryer, insert fryer basket, grease it with non-stick cooking oil spray, then shut with its lid, set the fryer at 400 degrees F, and preheat for 5 minutes.
2. Meanwhile, take a large bowl, place squash slices in it, add remaining ingredients and then toss until coated.
3. Open the fryer, arrange squash slices in the air fryer basket in a single layer, close with its lid and cook for 8 to 10 minutes until thoroughly cooked and golden brown, turning halfway.
4. Serve straight away.

Nutrition Value:

- Calories: 21 Cal
- Fat: 2.4 g
- Carbs: 0.2 g
- Protein: 0.2 g
- Fiber: 0.05 g

Falafel

Preparation time: 1 hour and 10 minutes
Cooking time: 35 minutes
Servings: 4

Ingredients:

For Falafels:

- 1 cup dried chickpeas, soaked overnight
- 3 tablespoons almond flour
- ¼ cup cilantro leaves
- 1 medium red onion, peeled, chopped
- 1 teaspoon minced garlic
- 3/4 teaspoon ground cumin
- 1/2 teaspoon baking powder
- 1/4 allspice
- 1 teaspoon ground coriander
- 3/4 teaspoon salt
- 2 tablespoons olive oil

For Tahini Yoghurt Sauce:

- 1 teaspoon tahini paste
- 1 lemon, juiced
- 1 tablespoon olive oil
- 1 cup Greek yogurt

Method:

1. Prepare yogurt sauce and for this, place all its ingredients in a bowl, whisk until well combined, and set aside until required.
2. Prepare falafels, and for this, place chickpeas in a food processor, add onion, garlic, and cilantro and pulse until ground.
3. Slowly blend in oil until incorporated, then tip the mixture in a bowl, add remaining ingredients, mix well and refrigerate for 1 hour.
4. Then switch on the air fryer, insert fryer basket, grease it with olive oil, then shut with its lid, set the fryer at 370 degrees F, and preheat for 5 minutes.
5. Meanwhile, prepare falafel balls and for this, roll falafel mixture into balls, 2 tablespoons of mixture per ball.
6. Open the fryer, add falafel balls in it in a single layer, spray with oil, close with its lid and cook for 15 minutes until nicely golden, crispy, and cooked through, shaking the basket halfway through.
7. When air fryer beeps, open its lid, transfer falafel onto a serving plate, cover with aluminum foil and cook remaining falafel balls in the same manner.
8. Serve falafel balls with prepared yogurt sauce.

Nutrition Value:

- Calories: 366 Cal
- Fat: 18 g
- Carbs: 40 g
- Protein: 15 g
- Fiber: 10 g

Spaghetti Squash

Preparation time: 5 minutes
Cooking time: 30 minutes
Servings: 4

Ingredients:

- 1 large spaghetti squash, halved, deseeded
- 1 teaspoon salt
- ½ teaspoon ground black pepper
- 1 teaspoon olive oil

Method:

1. Switch on the air fryer, insert fryer basket, grease it with non-stick cooking oil spray, then shut with its lid, set the fryer at 360 degrees F, and preheat for 5 minutes.
2. Meanwhile, brush the squash halves with oil and then season with salt and black pepper.
3. Open the fryer, arrange squash halves cut-side-up in the air fryer basket in a single layer, close with its lid and cook for 30minutes until thoroughly cooked.
4. Serve straight away.

Nutrition Value:

- Calories: 42 Cal
- Fat: 0.4 g
- Carbs: 10 g
- Protein: 1 g
- Fiber: 2.2 g

Spaghetti Squash Fritters

Preparation time: 10 minutes
Cooking time: 8 minutes
Servings: 4

Ingredients:

- 2 cups air-fried spaghetti squash
- ¼ cup coconut flour
- ½ teaspoon garlic powder
- 2 teaspoons sliced green onion
- 1 teaspoon dried parsley
- 1 egg
- 1 teaspoon olive oil

Method:

1. Switch on the air fryer, insert fryer basket, grease it with non-stick cooking oil spray, then shut with its lid, set the fryer at 400 degrees F, and preheat for 5 minutes.
2. Meanwhile, wrap air-fried spaghetti squash in a cheesecloth and then twist it well to remove excess water.
3. Take a large bowl, place spaghetti squash in it, add remaining ingredients, stir until combined and then shape the mixture into 4 evenly sized patties.
4. Open the fryer, arrange squash patties in the air fryer basket in a single layer, close with its lid and cook for 8 minutes until thoroughly cooked and golden brown, turning halfway.
5. Serve straight away.

Nutrition Value:

- Calories: 131 Cal
- Fat: 10.1 g
- Carbs: 5.1 g
- Protein: 3.8 g
- Fiber: 2 g

Brussels Sprouts

Preparation time: 10 minutes
Cooking time: 14 minutes
Servings: 4

Ingredients:

- 2 cups Brussels sprouts, cut into quarters
- 1/4 teaspoon sea salt
- 1 tablespoon olive oil

Method:

1. Switch on the air fryer, insert fryer basket, grease it with olive oil, then shut with its lid, set the fryer at 375 degrees F, and preheat for 5 minutes.
2. Meanwhile, place Brussel sprouts in a large bowl, drizzle with oil, and then season with salt and toss until well coated.
3. Open the fryer, add sprouts in it, close with its lid and cook for 9 minutes until nicely golden and crispy, shaking the basket every 5 minutes.
4. When air fryer beeps, open its lid, transfer sprouts onto a serving plate, and serve.

Nutrition Value:

- Calories: 50 Cal
- Fat: 4 g
- Carbs: 4 g
- Protein: 1 g
- Fiber: 2 g

Grilled Tomatoes

Preparation time: 5 minutes
Cooking time: 50 minutes
Servings: 2

Ingredients:

- 1 pound cherry tomatoes, halved height-wise

Method:

1. Switch on the air fryer, insert fryer basket, grease it with non-stick cooking oil spray, then shut with its lid, set the fryer at 240 degrees F, and preheat for 5 minutes.
2. Open the fryer, arrange tomato halves in the air fryer basket in a single layer, spray oil on the food, close with its lid and cook for 45 minutes until thoroughly cooked and half of their original size.
3. Then switch the temperature of air fryer to 390 degrees F and continue frying the tomatoes for 5 minutes.
4. Serve straight away.

Nutrition Value:

- Calories: 28.9 Cal
- Fat: 1.4 g
- Carbs: 2 g
- Protein: 0.4 g
- Fiber: 0.4 g

Veggie Quesadillas

Preparation time: 10 minutes
Cooking time: 25 minutes
Servings: 4

Ingredients:

- 1 cup sliced red bell pepper
- 1 cup cooked black beans
- 1 cup sliced zucchini
- 1/4 teaspoon ground cumin
- 1 teaspoon lime zest
- 1 tablespoon lime juice
- 2 tablespoons chopped cilantro
- 1 cup shredded cheddar cheese
- 2 ounces Greek yogurt
- 1/2 cup drained pico de gallo
- 4 whole-wheat flour tortillas, each about 6-inch

Method:

1. Prepare quesadilla and for this, place tortilla wraps on working space, sprinkle 2 tablespoons of cheddar over half of each wrap, top cheese with ¼ cup each of black beans, zucchini, and red pepper, and then top with remaining cheese.
2. Cover filling with the other half of tortillas, making a moon-shaped quesadilla, then secure with a toothpick and spray with oil.
3. Switch on the air fryer, insert fryer basket, grease it with olive oil, then shut with its lid, set the fryer at 400 degrees F, and preheat for 5 minutes.
4. Open the fryer, add quesadilla in it in a single layer, close with its lid and cook for 10 minutes until nicely golden, crispy, and vegetables have softened, turning quesadilla halfway through.
5. When air fryer beeps, open its lid, transfer quesadilla onto a serving plate, keep it warm and cook remaining quesadilla in the same manner.
6. Serve straight away.

Nutrition Value:

- Calories: 291 Cal
- Fat: 8 g
- Carbs: 36 g
- Protein: 17 g
- Fiber: 8 g

Buttermilk Fried Mushrooms

Preparation time: 20 minutes
Cooking time: 12 minutes
Servings: 2

Ingredients:

- 2 cups oyster mushrooms
- 1 teaspoon onion powder
- 1 teaspoon garlic powder
- 1 teaspoon salt
- 1 ½ cup coconut flour
- 1 teaspoon ground black pepper
- 1 teaspoon paprika
- 1 teaspoon ground cumin
- 1 cup buttermilk

Method:

1. Take a large bowl, place mushrooms in it, add milk, toss until coated and then let them marinate for 15 minutes.
2. When ready to cook, switch on the air fryer, insert fryer basket, grease it with non-stick cooking oil spray, then shut with its lid, set the fryer at 375 degrees F, and preheat for 5 minutes.
3. Meanwhile, take a large bowl, place flour in it, add all the spices and then stir until mixed.
4. Working on one mushroom at a time, remove it from buttermilk, dredge into the flour mixture, dip into the buttermilk and then dredge again into the flour mixture until coated.
5. Open the fryer, arrange mushrooms in the air fryer basket in a single layer, spray oil on the food, close with its lid and cook for 12 minutes until thoroughly cooked, turning halfway.
6. Serve straight away.

Nutrition Value:

- Calories: 355 Cal
- Fat: 9.7 g
- Carbs: 57 g
- Protein: 12.4 g
- Fiber: 3 g

Roasted Turnips

Preparation time: 5 minutes
Cooking time: 25 minutes
Servings: 4

Ingredients:

- 4 medium turnips, peeled, diced
- 1 teaspoon sea salt
- 1 ½ teaspoon paprika
- 1 teaspoon ground black pepper
- 2 teaspoons olive oil
- 2 teaspoons minced parsley

Method:

1. Switch on the air fryer, insert fryer basket, grease it with non-stick cooking oil spray, then shut with its lid, set the fryer at 390 degrees F, and preheat for 5 minutes.
2. Meanwhile, take a medium bowl, place turnips pieces in it, add remaining ingredients except for the parsley and then stir until combined.
3. Open the fryer, arrange turnip pieces in the air fryer basket in a single layer, close with its lid and cook for 25 minutes until thoroughly cooked and golden brown, turning halfway.
4. Serve straight away.

Nutrition Value:

- Calories: 51 Cal
- Fat: 3 g
- Carbs: 9 g
- Protein: 1 g
- Fiber: 3 g

Artichoke Hearts

Preparation time: 5 minutes
Cooking time: 8 minutes
Servings: 4

Ingredients:

- 14 ounces canned artichoke hearts, quarter, drained
- 1/8 teaspoon garlic powder
- ¼ teaspoon salt
- 1/8 teaspoon ground black pepper
- ¼ teaspoon Italian seasoning
- 2 teaspoons vegan grated parmesan cheese
- 1 tablespoon olive oil

Method:

1. Switch on the air fryer, insert fryer basket, grease it with non-stick cooking oil spray, then shut with its lid, set the fryer at 390 degrees F, and preheat for 5 minutes.
2. Meanwhile, pat dry the artichoke hearts, place them in a large bowl, add remaining ingredients and then toss until coated.
3. Open the fryer, arrange artichoke hearts in the air fryer basket in a single layer, close with its lid and cook for 8 minutes until thoroughly cooked and golden brown, turning halfway.
4. Serve straight away.

Nutrition Value:

- Calories: 67 Cal
- Fat: 3.7 g
- Carbs: 6.6 g
- Protein: 2.6 g
- Fiber: 2.2 g

Ginger Soy Tofu

Preparation time: 15 minutes
Cooking time: 60 minutes
Servings: 4

Ingredients:

For Tofu:

- 14 ounces tofu, pressed, drained
- 1 teaspoon garlic powder
- 1/2 teaspoon smoked paprika
- 1/4 cup arrowroot flour
- 1 teaspoon salt
- 1/2 teaspoon ground cumin

For Gingery Soy Sauce:

- 1 teaspoon garlic powder
- 2 tablespoons agave nectar
- 1 tablespoon grated ginger
- 1/4 teaspoon ground black pepper
- 3 tablespoons soy sauce
- 1 tablespoon coconut oil
- 2 tablespoons coconut sugar
- 1 teaspoon white sesame seeds
- 1 scallion, chopped

Method:

1. Switch on the air fryer, insert fryer basket, grease it with olive oil, then shut with its lid, set the fryer at 350 degrees F, and preheat for 10 minutes.
2. Meanwhile, cut tofu in slices, cut each slice into eight squares, and place tofu pieces in a plastic bag.
3. Add remaining ingredients, seal the bag, and shake well until well coated.
4. Open the fryer, add tofu pieces in it in a single layer, spray with olive oil, close with its lid and cook for 25 minutes until nicely golden and crispy, shaking the basket every 5 minutes and turning halfway through.
5. Meanwhile, prepare the sauce and for this, place all its ingredients in a large bowl except for sesame seeds and scallion and whisk until combined, set aside until required.
6. When air fryer beeps, open its lid, transfer tofu pieces to plate, keep them warm, and cook remaining tofu pieces in the same manner.
7. When done, transfer tofu pieces to the bowl containing prepared sauce and toss until coated.
8. Garnish tofu with sesame seeds and scallion and then serve.

Nutrition Value:

- Calories: 139 Cal
- Fat: 4.4 g
- Carbs: 17.8 g
- Protein: 10.3 g
- Fiber: 1.6 g

Loaded Potatoes

Preparation time: 10 minutes
Cooking time: 30 minutes
Servings: 4

Ingredients:

- 11 ounces baby potatoes
- 2 slices of bacon, center-cut
- 1 1/2 tablespoons chopped chives
- 1/8 teaspoon salt
- 1 teaspoon olive oil
- 2 tablespoons shredded Cheddar cheese
- 2 tablespoons sour cream

Method:

1. Switch on the air fryer, insert fryer basket, grease it with olive oil, then shut with its lid, set the fryer at 350 degrees F, and preheat for 5 minutes.
2. Meanwhile, place potatoes in a bowl, drizzle with oil and toss until coated.
3. Open the fryer, add potatoes in it, close with its lid and cook for 25 minutes until nicely golden, crispy and fork-tender, shaking the basket every 5 minutes and turning potatoes halfway through.
4. In the meantime, take a skillet pan, place it over medium heat, add bacon, cook for 7 minutes or until crispy, then transfer it to a cutting board and crumble it.
5. When air fryer beeps, open its lid, transfer potatoes onto a serving plate, lightly crush them and then drizzle with bacon dripping.
6. Season potatoes with salt, top with sour cream and chives, sprinkle with chives and bacon, and serve.

Nutrition Value:

- Calories: 199 Cal
- Fat: 7 g
- Carbs: 26 g
- Protein: 7 g
- Fiber: 4 g

Cauliflower Wings

Preparation time: 10 minutes
Cooking time: 18 minutes
Servings: 4

Ingredients:

- 1 large head of cauliflower, cut into florets
- 1 teaspoon cornstarch
- 1 teaspoon onion powder
- 1 teaspoon garlic salt
- 1 cup coconut flour
- ½ teaspoon salt
- 1 teaspoon smoked paprika
- 1 teaspoon white vinegar
- ½ teaspoon ground black pepper
- 2 tablespoons vegan butter, melted
- ½ cup Buffalo Sauce
- 1 cup almond milk, unsweetened

Method:

1. Switch on the air fryer, insert fryer basket, grease it with non-stick cooking oil spray, then shut with its lid, set the fryer at 400 degrees F, and preheat for 5 minutes.
2. Meanwhile, take a medium saucepan, place it over medium heat, pour in milk, whisk in cornstarch until smooth and then cook the mixture for 5 minutes until slightly thickened.
3. Meanwhile, take a large bowl, place flour in it, add garlic salt, onion powder, salt, black pepper and paprika and then stir until mixed.
4. Working on one floret at a time, dredge in flour mixture, dip in milk mixture and then dredge in flour mixture until coated.
5. Open the fryer, arrange the cauliflower florets in the air fryer basket in a single layer, spray oil on the food, close with its lid and cook for 8 minutes until thoroughly cooked and golden brown, turning halfway.
6. Meanwhile, prepare the sauce and for this, take a small saucepan, place it over medium heat, add butter, vinegar and buffalo sauce, whisk until combined and then cook until butter melts and sauce begin to simmer.
7. When cauliflower florets have fried, toss them into the prepared sauce and then serve.

Nutrition Value:

- Calories: 357 Cal
- Fat: 18.8 g
- Carbs: 39.4 g
- Protein: 10.6 g
- Fiber: 6.5 g

Brussels Sprouts

Preparation time: 5 minutes
Cooking time: 14 minutes
Servings: 2

Ingredients:

- 2 cups Brussels sprouts
- ¼ teaspoon sea salt
- 1 tablespoon balsamic vinegar
- 1 tablespoon olive oil

Method:

1. Switch on the air fryer, insert fryer basket, grease it with non-stick cooking oil spray, then shut with its lid, set the fryer at 400 degrees F, and preheat for 5 minutes.
2. Meanwhile, take a large bowl, place all the ingredients in it and then toss until mixed.
3. Open the fryer, arrange the Brussels sprouts in the air fryer basket in a single layer, close with its lid and cook for 14 minutes until thoroughly cooked and golden brown, turning halfway.
4. Serve straight away.

Nutrition Value:

- Calories: 212.7 Cal
- Fat: 6.9 g
- Carbs: 24.2 g
- Protein: 5.8 g
- Fiber: 9.8 g

Eggplant

Preparation time: 10 minutes
Cooking time: 20 minutes
Servings: 4

Ingredients:

- 1 ½ pound eggplant, ½-inch cubed
- 1 teaspoon garlic powder
- 1 tablespoon salt
- ½ teaspoon dried oregano
- ¼ teaspoon ground black pepper
- ¼ teaspoon dried thyme
- 1 teaspoon paprika
- 2 tablespoons vegetable broth

Method:

1. Place eggplant pieces in a colander, sprinkle with salt, toss until mixed and then let them rest for 30 minutes.
2. Then drain the eggplant pieces, pat dry with paper towels and place in a large bowl.
3. Add remaining ingredients into a large bowl and then toss until mixed.
4. Switch on the air fryer, insert fryer basket, grease it with non-stick cooking oil spray, then shut with its lid, set the fryer at 380 degrees F, and preheat for 5 minutes.
5. Open the fryer, arrange the eggplant pieces in the air fryer basket, spray oil on the food, close with its lid and cook for 20 minutes until thoroughly cooked and golden brown, turning halfway.
6. Serve straight away.

Nutrition Value:

- Calories: 48 Cal
- Fat: 1 g
- Carbs: 11 g
- Protein: 2 g
- Fiber: 5 g

Chapter 7: Fish and Seafood

Fish Sticks

Preparation time: 10 minutes
Cooking time: 25 minutes
Servings: 4

Ingredients:

- 1 pound cod fillets
- 1 1/2 cups pork rind panko
- 2 tablespoons Dijon mustard
- ½ teaspoon ground black pepper
- 2/3 teaspoon salt
- ¾ teaspoon Cajun seasoning
- 2 tablespoons water
- 1/4 cup mayonnaise

Method:

1. Prepare fish sticks and for this, pat dry cod fillets, then cut them into 1 by 2 inches wide sticks and set aside until required.
2. Place mayonnaise in a bowl, add water and mustard and whisk until combined.
3. Place pork rinds in a shallow dish, add Cajun seasoning, season with salt and black pepper and stir until mixed.
4. First, dip each fish stick into the mayonnaise mixture, then dredge with pork rind mixture, place it on a plate, and coat remaining fish sticks in the same manner.
5. Switch on the air fryer, insert fryer basket, grease it with olive oil, then shut with its lid, set the fryer at 400 degrees F, and preheat for 5 minutes.
6. Open the fryer, add fish sticks in it in a single layer, spray with olive oil, close with its lid and cook for 10 minutes until nicely golden and crispy, shaking the basket every 5 minutes and filling the fish sticks halfway through.
7. When air fryer beeps, open its lid, transfer fish sticks onto a serving plate, keep them warm and cook remaining fish sticks in the same manner.
8. Serve straight away.

Nutrition Value:

- Calories: 263 Cal
- Fat: 16 g
- Carbs: 1 g
- Protein: 26.4 g
- Fiber: 0.5 g

Lemon and Garlic Salmon

Preparation time: 5 minutes
Cooking time: 14 minutes
Servings: 4

Ingredients:

- 4 fillets of salmon, each about 6 ounces
- 1 lemon, cut into slices
- 1 teaspoon sea salt
- 2 teaspoons garlic powder
- 2 teaspoons Italian seasoning
- 1 teaspoon ground black pepper
- 2 tablespoons olive oil
- 1 teaspoon lemon juice

Method:

1. Switch on the air fryer, insert fryer basket, grease it with non-stick cooking oil spray, then shut with its lid, set the fryer at 400 degrees F, and preheat for 5 minutes.
2. Meanwhile, prepare the salmon and for this, rub with oil and lemon juice and then season with salt, black pepper and Italian seasoning
3. Open the fryer, arrange salmon in the air fryer basket, scatter lemon slices on top, spray oil on the food, close with its lid and cook for 14 minutes until thoroughly cooked.
4. Serve straight away.

Nutrition Value:

- Calories: 462 Cal
- Fat: 28 g
- Carbs: 13 g
- Protein: 39 g
- Fiber: 2 g

Blackened Fish Lettuce Wrap

Preparation time: 5 minutes
Cooking time: 10 minutes
Servings: 4

Ingredients:

- 1 pound Mahi-Mahi fillets
- 2 ½ tablespoon Cajun seasoning
- 2 tablespoons olive oil

For Serving:

- 4 large lettuce leaves
- ½ cup mango salsa
- ½ cup shredded cabbage

Method:

1. Switch on the air fryer, insert fryer basket, grease it with non-stick cooking oil spray, then shut with its lid, set the fryer at 360 degrees F, and preheat for 5 minutes.
2. Meanwhile, prepare the fish and for this, brush the fillets with oil and then season with the Cajun seasoning until coated.
3. Open the fryer, arrange fillets in the air fryer basket, spray oil on the food, close with its lid and cook for 10 minutes until thoroughly cooked and golden brown, turning halfway.
4. When done, evenly divide Mahi-Mahi fillets among the lettuce leaves, top with mango salsa and cabbage and then serve.

Nutrition Value:

- Calories: 247 Cal
- Fat: 3 g
- Carbs: 32 g
- Protein: 25 g
- Fiber: 5 g

Fish Skewers

Preparation time: 35 minutes
Cooking time: 8 minutes
Servings: 4

Ingredients:

- 2 fillets of salmon, 1-inch cubed
- 1 medium red bell pepper, cored, cubed
- 1 medium orange bell pepper, cored, cubed
- 1 medium green bell pepper, cored, cubed

For the Marinade:

- 2 teaspoons minced garlic
- 1 teaspoon salt
- 2 teaspoons dried thyme
- ½ teaspoon ground black pepper
- 2 teaspoons dried oregano
- 1 teaspoon ground cumin
- ½ cup olive oil
- ½ teaspoon ground coriander
- 2 tablespoons lemon juice

Method:

1. Take a small bowl, place all the ingredients for the marinade in it and then stir until combined.
2. Take a large plastic bag
3. pour the marinade mixture in it, and then add salmon pieces and vegetable pieces in it.
4. Seal the bag
5. turn it upside down until salmon and vegetable pieces are coated in marinate and then marinate in the refrigerator for a minimum of 30 minutes.
6. When ready to cook, switch on the air fryer, insert the fryer basket, grease it with non-stick cooking oil spray, then shut with its lid, set the fryer at 350 degrees F, and preheat for 5 minutes.
7. Meanwhile, thread salmon pieces and vegetable pieces into the wooden skewers.
8. Open the fryer, arrange skewers in the air fryer basket in a single layer, spray oil on the food, close with its lid and cook for 6 to 8 minutes until thoroughly cooked, turning halfway.

9. Serve straight away.

Nutrition Value:

- Calories: 255.4 Cal
- Fat: 6.2 g
- Carbs: 12 g
- Protein: 30.2 g
- Fiber: 2.8 g

Lemon Pepper Shrimp

Preparation time: 5 minutes
Cooking time: 8 minutes
Servings: 2

Ingredients:

- 12 ounces shrimp, peeled, deveined
- ¼ teaspoon garlic powder
- 1 teaspoon lemon pepper
- 1 lemon, juiced
- ¼ teaspoon paprika
- 1 tablespoon olive oil

Method:

1. Switch on the air fryer, insert fryer basket, grease it with non-stick cooking oil spray, then shut with its lid, set the fryer at 400 degrees F, and preheat for 5 minutes.
2. Meanwhile, take a large bowl, place all the ingredients in it and then stir until well combined.
3. Open the fryer, arrange shrimps in the air fryer basket in a single layer, close with its lid and cook for 6 to 8 minutes until thoroughly cooked, turning halfway.
4. Serve straight away.

Nutrition Value:

- Calories: 215 Cal
- Fat: 8.6 g
- Carbs: 12.6 g
- Protein: 28.6 g
- Fiber: 5.5 g

Tomato Basil Scallops

Preparation time: 10 minutes
Cooking time: 20 minutes
Servings: 2

Ingredients:

- 8 jumbo sea scallops
- 12 ounces frozen spinach, thawed, drained
- 1 tablespoon chopped basil
- 1 tablespoon tomato paste
- 1 teaspoon minced garlic
- 1/2 teaspoon salt and more as needed
- 1/2 teaspoon ground black pepper and more as needed
- 2 tablespoons olive oil
- 3/4 cup heavy whipping cream

Method:

1. Switch on the air fryer, then shut with its lid, set the fryer at 350 degrees F, and preheat for 10 minutes.
2. Meanwhile, take an air fryer baking pan and then line spinach evenly in the bottom.
3. Place scallops in a bowl, drizzle with oil, season with salt and black pepper, toss until coated, and then top them over spinach.
4. Place tomato paste in a bowl, add garlic, basil, ¼ teaspoon each of salt and black pepper, and cream, whisk until mixed and then spread the mixture over scallops.
5. Open the fryer, insert baking pan in it, close with its lid and cook for 10 minutes until thoroughly cooked and sauce is bubbling.
6. When air fryer beeps, open its lid, take out the baking pan, transfer spinach and scallops onto a serving plate and serve.

Nutrition Value:

- Calories: 359 Cal
- Fat: 33 g
- Carbs: 6 g
- Protein: 9 g
- Fiber: 2 g

Catfish with Green Beans

Preparation time: 10 minutes
Cooking time: 25 minutes
Servings: 2

Ingredients:

- 2 catfish fillets, each about 6-ounces
- 12 ounces fresh green beans, trimmed
- 3/8 teaspoon salt, divided
- 1/4 teaspoon ground black pepper
- 1/2 teaspoon crushed red pepper
- 1 1/2 teaspoon chopped dill
- 1 teaspoon swerve sweetener
- 1/8 teaspoon coconut sugar
- 1/4 cup almond flour
- 1/3 cup panko breadcrumbs
- 2 tablespoons olive oil
- 1/2 teaspoon apple cider vinegar
- 1 egg, beaten
- 3/4 teaspoon dill pickle relish
- 2 tablespoons mayonnaise
- Lemon wedges for serving

Method:

1. Switch on the air fryer, insert fryer basket, grease it with olive oil, then shut with its lid, set the fryer at 400 degrees F, and preheat for 5 minutes.
2. Meanwhile, take a medium bowl, add green beans in it, drizzle with oil, season with 1/8 teaspoon salt, red pepper, and sweetener and toss until coated.
3. Open the fryer, add green beans in it, close with its lid and cook for 12 minutes until nicely golden brown and tender, shaking the basket every 5 minutes.
4. In the meantime, dredge fish fillets with almond flour, then dip in beaten egg and coat with panko bread crumbs, pressing them lightly into the fillets.
5. When air fryer beeps, open its lid, transfer green beans onto a serving plate, wrap with foil to keep them warm, and set aside until required.
6. Add prepared fillets into the fryer basket, spray them with olive oil, and continue cooking for 8 minutes until nicely golden brown and thoroughly cooked.
7. Prepare dip and for this, place mayonnaise in a bowl, add sugar, dill, vinegar, and relish and stir until mixed.
8. When done, season fillets with remaining salt and black pepper and serve with green beans, prepared dip and lemon wedges.

Nutrition Value:

- Calories: 416 Cal
- Fat: 18 g
- Carbs: 31 g
- Protein: 33 g
- Fiber: 12 g

Garlic Lime Shrimp

Preparation time: 10 minutes
Cooking time: 8 minutes
Servings: 2

Ingredients:

- 1 cup fresh shrimps, peeled, deveined, cleaned
- ½ teaspoon minced garlic
- 1/8 teaspoon ground black pepper
- 1 lime, juiced
- 1/8 teaspoon salt
- 5 wooden skewers, each about 6-inch, soaked

Method:

1. Switch on the air fryer, insert fryer basket, grease it with olive oil, then shut with its lid, set the fryer at 220 degrees F, and preheat for 10 minutes.
2. Meanwhile, place shrimps in a bowl, season with salt and black pepper, add garlic and lime juice, toss until well mixed and then thread them onto the skewers.
3. Open the fryer, add shrimps in it in a single layer, close with its lid and cook for 8 minutes until nicely golden and cooked through, turning shrimps halfway through.
4. When air fryer beeps, open its lid, transfer shrimps onto a serving plate, and serve.

Nutrition Value:

- Calories: 76 Cal
- Fat: 1 g
- Carbs: 4 g
- Protein: 13 g
- Fiber: 0 g

Salmon and Asparagus

Preparation time: 10 minutes
Cooking time: 18 minutes
Servings: 2

Ingredients:

- 2 salmon fillets, deboned, each about 6 ounces
- 2 tablespoons dill
- 1 bunch of asparagus
- 2 tablespoons chopped parsley
- ½ teaspoon salt
- ½ teaspoon ground black pepper
- 1 tablespoon olive oil
- 1 1/2 tablespoons lemon juice

Method:

1. Switch on the air fryer, insert fryer basket, grease it with olive oil, then shut with its lid, set the fryer at 400 degrees F, and preheat for 10 minutes.
2. Meanwhile, place lemon juice and olive oil, add salt, black pepper, parsley, and dill and stir until mixed.
3. Prepare salmon, and for this, coat the leash of each fillet with ¾ of parsley mixture.
4. Place asparagus in another bowl, add reserved parsley mixture, and toss until combined.
5. Open the fryer, spread asparagus in the bottom, top with salmon, spray with olive oil, close with its lid and cook for 8 minutes until nicely golden and cooked through, turning salmon halfway through.
6. When air fryer beeps, open its lid, transfer salmon and asparagus onto a serving plate and serve.

Nutrition Value:

- Calories: 391 Cal
- Fat: 19 g
- Carbs: 9 g
- Protein: 48 g
- Fiber: 5 g

Fish Cakes with Cilantro

Preparation time: 5 minutes
Cooking time: 10 minutes
Servings: 2

Ingredients:

- 2/3 cup oats
- 10 ounces chopped catfish
- ¼ teaspoon salt
- 2 tablespoons sweet chili sauce
- ¼ teaspoon ground black pepper
- 2 tablespoons vegan mayonnaise
- 3 tablespoons chopped cilantro
- 1 egg

Method:

1. Switch on the air fryer, insert fryer basket, grease it with non-stick cooking oil spray, then shut with its lid, set the fryer at 400 degrees F, and preheat for 5 minutes.
2. Meanwhile, take a large bowl, place all the ingredients in it, stir until combined and then shape the mixture into four evenly sized patties.
3. Open the fryer, arrange fish cakes in the air fryer basket in a single layer, spray oil on the food, close with its lid and cook for 10 minutes until thoroughly cooked and golden brown, turning halfway.
4. Serve straight away.

Nutrition Value:

- Calories: 399 Cal
- Fat: 15.5 g
- Carbs: 27.9 g
- Protein: 34.6 g
- Fiber: 2.8 g

Pecan Crusted Halibut

Preparation time: 10 minutes
Cooking time: 8 minutes
Servings: 4

Ingredients:

- 4 fillets of halibut, skinless, each about 4 ounces
- ½ cup pecans, ground
- ½ cup corn starch
- ½ cup oats
- 3 tablespoons lemon pepper seasoning
- 2 egg whites
- ½ cup white wine

Method:

1. Switch on the air fryer, insert fryer basket, grease it with non-stick cooking oil spray, then shut with its lid, set the fryer at 375 degrees F, and preheat for 5 minutes.
2. Meanwhile, take a medium bowl, place the egg whites in it, and then whisk in cornstarch until blended.
3. Whisk in wine until well combined, and then whisk in 1 ½ tablespoon lemon pepper seasoning until smooth batter comes together.
4. Take a shallow dish and then place oats in it.
5. Working on one halibut fillet at a time, season it with salt and lemon pepper, dip into the prepared egg whites mixture and then dredge in pecan until coated.
6. Open the fryer, arrange halibut fillets in the air fryer basket in a single layer, spray oil on the food, close with its lid and cook for 10 minutes until thoroughly cooked and golden brown, turning halfway.
7. Serve straight away.

Nutrition Value:

- Calories: 432 Cal
- Fat: 16 g
- Carbs: 31 g
- Protein: 37 g
- Fiber: 3 g

Parmesan Shrimp

Preparation time: 5 minutes
Cooking time: 25 minutes
Servings: 4

Ingredients:

- 2 pounds jumbo shrimp, peeled, deveined, cooked
- 2 teaspoons minced garlic
- 1/2 teaspoon dried oregano
- 1 teaspoon ground black pepper
- 1 teaspoon dried basil
- 1 teaspoon onion powder
- 2/3 cup grated parmesan cheese
- 2 tablespoons olive oil
- 1 lemon, quartered

Method:

1. Switch on the air fryer, insert fryer basket, grease it with olive oil, then shut with its lid, set the fryer at 350 degrees F, and preheat for 5 minutes.
2. Meanwhile, place all the ingredients in a bowl and toss until well mixed and coated.
3. Open the fryer, add shrimps in it in a single layer, close with its lid and cook for 10 minutes until nicely golden brown and cooked through, turning shrimps halfway through.
4. When air fryer beeps, open its lid, transfer shrimps onto a serving plate, keep them warm and cook remaining shrimps in the same manner.
5. Serve straight away.

Nutrition Value:

- Calories: 307.7 Cal
- Fat: 16.4 g
- Carbs: 12.2 g
- Protein: 27.6 g
- Fiber: 3 g

Cod

Preparation time: 5 minutes
Cooking time: 16 minutes
Servings: 6

Ingredients:

- 1 ½ pound cod, skinless, about 6 pieces
- ½ teaspoon salt
- ½ teaspoon garlic powder
- 1 teaspoon smoked paprika
- 1/8 teaspoon ground black pepper
- 2 teaspoon old bay seasoning
- ½ cup oats

Method:

1. Switch on the air fryer, insert fryer basket, grease it with non-stick cooking oil spray, then shut with its lid, set the fryer at 390 degrees F, and preheat for 5 minutes.
2. Meanwhile, take a shallow dish, place all the ingredients except for the cod pieces and then stir until mixed.
3. Working on one fish piece at a time, dredge it in oats mixture until coated.
4. Open the fryer, arrange the cod pieces in the air fryer basket in a single layer, spray oil on the food, close with its lid and cook for 16 minutes until thoroughly cooked, turning halfway.
5. Serve straight away.

Nutrition Value:

- Calories: 70 Cal
- Fat: 1 g
- Carbs: 15 g
- Protein: 2 g
- Fiber: 1 g

Salmon Cakes

Preparation time: 5 minutes
Cooking time: 30 minutes
Servings: 2

Ingredients:

- 15 ounces canned salmon, without bones and skin
- 1 teaspoon salt
- ½ cup oats
- ¼ teaspoon ground black pepper
- 2 tablespoons chopped dill
- 2 teaspoons mustard paste
- 1 egg
- 2 tablespoons vegan mayonnaise

Method:

1. Switch on the air fryer, insert fryer basket, grease it with non-stick cooking oil spray, then shut with its lid, set the fryer at 390 degrees F, and preheat for 5 minutes.
2. Meanwhile, take a large bowl, place salmon in it, add remaining ingredients and then shape the mixture into four evenly sized patties.
3. Open the fryer, arrange salmon patties in the air fryer basket in a single layer, spray oil on the food, close with its lid and cook for 12 minutes until thoroughly cooked and golden brown, turning halfway.
4. Serve straight away.

Nutrition Value:

- Calories: 517 Cal
- Fat: 26.7 g
- Carbs: 14.7 g
- Protein: 51.8 g
- Fiber: 2.1 g

Shrimp Scampi

Preparation time: 10 minutes
Cooking time: 7 minutes
Servings: 4

Ingredients:

- 25 shrimps, defrosted, peeled, deveined, cleaned
- 1 tablespoon minced garlic
- 1 teaspoon dried basil
- 2 teaspoons red pepper flakes
- 1 teaspoon dried chives
- 4 tablespoons unsalted butter
- 1 tablespoon lemon juice
- 2 tablespoons chicken stock

Method:

1. Switch on the air fryer, insert fryer baking pan, grease it with olive oil, then shut with its lid, set the fryer at 330 degrees F, and preheat for 5 minutes.
2. Open the fryer, add garlic, red pepper, and butter in it, close with its lid and cook for 2 minutes until the butter has melted.
3. Then add remaining ingredients into the baking pan, stir gently, shut the air fryer with lid and continue cooking for 5 minutes until shrimps have cooked through.
4. When air fryer beeps, open its lid, take out the baking pan and let shrimps rest for 1 minute.
5. Stir the shrimps, transfer them to a plate and serve.

Nutrition Value:

- Calories: 221 Cal
- Fat: 13 g
- Carbs: 1 g
- Protein: 23 g
- Fiber: 0 g

Chapter 8: Dessert

Spiced Apples

Preparation time: 5 minutes
Cooking time: 12 minutes
Servings: 4

Ingredients:

- 4 small apples, cored, sliced
- 1 teaspoon apple pie spice
- 2 tablespoons coconut sugar
- 2 tablespoons coconut oil, melted
- 4 tablespoons whipped topping

Method:

1. Switch on the air fryer, insert baking basket, grease it with olive oil, then shut with its lid, set the fryer at 350 degrees F, and preheat for 5 minutes.
2. Meanwhile, place apple slices in a bowl, drizzle with oil, sprinkle with sugar and apple pie spice and toss until well coated.
3. Open the fryer, add apple pieces in the baking pan, close with its lid and cook for 12 minutes until tender, shaking the basket every 5 minutes.
4. When air fryer beeps, open its lid, take out the baking pan, transfer apple to a serving plate, top with whipped topping, and serve.

Nutrition Value:

- Calories: 233 Cal
- Fat: 10.6 g
- Carbs: 32.6 g
- Protein: 1.7 g
- Fiber: 3.6 g

Churros

Preparation time: 1 hour and 15 minutes
Cooking time: 35 minutes
Servings: 4

Ingredients:

- 1/3 cup unsalted butter
- 1 cup almond flour
- 1/2 cup coconut sugar
- 2 tablespoons erythritol sweetener
- 1/4 teaspoon salt
- 3/4 teaspoon ground cinnamon
- 1 teaspoon vanilla extract, unsweetened
- 2 eggs
- 1 cup of water

Method:

1. Cut butter into cubes, place it into a saucepan, then place it over medium-high heat, add salt, sweetener, and water and bring the mixture to boil.
2. Switch heat to medium-low level, add flour and stir it continuously until a smooth dough comes together.
3. Remove pan from heat, then transfer the dough to a bowl and let cool for 5 minutes.
4. Add eggs and vanilla, mix with an electric mixture until dough comes together, and then transfer the dough into a large piping bag with a star-shaped tip.
5. Take a baking sheet, grease it with olive oil, then pipe churros on it, about 4-inch long and cutting the ends with a scissor, and then refrigerate for 1 hour.
6. Then switch on the air fryer, insert fryer basket, grease it with olive oil, then shut with its lid, set the fryer at 375 degrees F, and preheat for 5 minutes.
7. Open the fryer, add churros in it in a single layer, ½-inch apart, spray with olive oil, close with its lid, and cook for 12 minutes until nicely golden, shaking the basket every 5 minutes.
8. Meanwhile, place coconut sugar in a large bowl, add cinnamon in it, stir until mixed and set aside until required.
9. When air fryer beeps, open its lid, transfer churros into the bowl containing cinnamon-sugar mixture, toss until coated, and cook remaining churros in the same manner.
10. Serve straight away.

Nutrition Value:

- Calories: 442.5 Cal
- Fat: 31 g
- Carbs: 33.2 g
- Protein: 9 g
- Fiber: 3.3 g

Fruit Crumble Mug Cakes

Preparation time: 5 minutes
Cooking time: 20 minutes
Servings: 4

Ingredients:

- 1 small peach, cored, diced
- 4 plums, pitted, diced
- 2 tablespoons oats
- 1 small apple, cored, diced
- 4 ounces almond flour
- 1 small pear, diced
- 2 tablespoons swerve caster sugar
- 1 ¾ tablespoon coconut sugar
- 1 tablespoon honey
- 2 ounces unsalted butter
- ¼ cup blueberries, diced

Method:

1. Switch on the air fryer, insert fryer basket, grease it with olive oil, then shut with its lid, set the fryer at 320 degrees F, and preheat for 5 minutes.
2. Meanwhile, take four heatproof mugs or ramekins, evenly fill them with fruits, and then cover with coconut sugar and honey.
3. Place flour in a bowl, add butter and caster sugar, then rub with fingers until the mixture resembled crumbs, then stir in oats and evenly spoon this mixture into prepared fruit mugs.
4. Open the fryer, place fruit mugs in it, close with its lid, cook for 10 minutes, then increase air fryer temperature to 390 degrees F and continue cooking for 5 minutes until the top have nicely browned and crunchy.
5. When air fryer beeps, open its lid, carefully take out the mugs and serve straight away.

Nutrition Value:

- Calories: 380 Cal
- Fat: 11 g
- Carbs: 68 g
- Protein: 5 g
- Fiber: 5 g

Banana Bread

Preparation time: 10 minutes
Cooking time: 45 minutes
Servings: 4

Ingredients:

- 3/4 cup whole wheat flour
- 3/4 cup mashed bananas
- 1/2 teaspoon salt
- 1 teaspoon cinnamon
- 2 tablespoons toasted walnuts, chopped
- 1/2 cup coconut sugar
- 1/4 teaspoon baking soda
- 1 teaspoon vanilla extract, unsweetened
- 2 tablespoons olive oil
- 1/3 cup Greek yogurt
- 2 eggs, beaten

Method:

1. Switch on the air fryer, insert fryer basket, then shut with its lid, set the fryer at 310 degrees F, and preheat for 10 minutes.
2. Meanwhile, take a 6-inch round cake pan, line it with parchment paper, spray with olive oil and set aside until required.
3. Place flour in a bowl, add salt, cinnamon, and baking soda and stir until mixed.
4. Crack eggs in another bowl, add mashed banana, coconut sugar, vanilla, yogurt, and oil and whisk well until incorporated.
5. Slowly whisk egg-banana mixture into the flour mixture until well combined, and smooth batter comes together, then spoon the batter into the prepared cake pan and top with walnuts.
6. Open the fryer, place cake pan in it, close with its lid, and cook for 30 to 35 minutes until top is nicely golden and the cake has thoroughly cooked.
7. When air fryer beeps, open its lid, take out the cake pan, then transfer cake to the wire rack and cool for 15 minutes.
8. Cut cake into slices and serve.

Nutrition Value:

- Calories: 180 Cal
- Fat: 6 g
- Carbs: 29 g
- Protein: 4 g
- Fiber: 2 g

Apple Chips

Preparation time: 5 minutes
Cooking time: 15 minutes
Servings: 6

Ingredients:

- 6 large red apples
- 1/8 teaspoon ground cinnamon
- 1 teaspoon olive oil

Method:

1. Switch on the air fryer, insert fryer basket, grease it with olive oil, then shut with its lid, set the fryer at 350 degrees F, and preheat for 5 minutes.
2. Meanwhile, place core each apple, cut into wedges, then place them in a bowl, drizzle with oil and toss until coated.
3. Open the fryer, add apple wedges in it, close with its lid and cook for 10 minutes until nicely golden and crispy, shaking the basket every 5 minutes.
4. When air fryer beeps, open its lid, transfer apple chips onto a serving plate, sprinkle with cinnamon, and serve.

Nutrition Value:

- Calories: 608 Cal
- Fat: 6 g
- Carbs: 150 g
- Protein: 2 g
- Fiber: 26 g

Cheesecake Bites

Preparation time: 40 minutes
Cooking time: 12 minutes
Servings: 2

Ingredients:

- 1/2 cup almond flour
- 1/2 cup and 2 tablespoons erythritol sweetener
- 1/2 teaspoon vanilla extract, unsweetened
- 8 ounces cream cheese, softened
- 4 tablespoons heavy cream, divided

Method:

1. Place softened cream cheese in the bowl of a stand mixer, add 2 tablespoons of cream and ½ cup sweetener and mix until blended and smooth.
2. Take a baking sheet, line it with a baking sheet, place cream cheese mixture on it, spread evenly, and place it into the freezer for a minimum of 30 minutes until firm.
3. Then switch on the air fryer, insert fryer basket, grease it with olive oil, then shut with its lid, set the fryer at 300 degrees F, and preheat for 5 minutes.
4. Meanwhile, place almond flour in a shallow dish, add remaining sweetener and stir until mixed.
5. Cut frozen cheesecake into bite-size pieces, then dip into remaining heavy cream and dredge with almond flour mixture until well coated.
6. Open the fryer, add cheesecake bites in it in a single layer, close with its lid and cook for 2 minutes until nicely golden and crispy.
7. When air fryer beeps, open its lid, transfer cheesecake bites onto a serving plate and cook remaining cheese bites in the same manner.
8. Serve straight away.

Nutrition Value:

- Calories: 329.3 Cal
- Fat: 30.7 g
- Carbs: 6.6 g
- Protein: 6.6 g
- Fiber: 1.5 g

Grilled Pineapple

Preparation time: 10 minutes
Cooking time: 28 minutes
Servings: 4

Ingredients:

- 1 medium pineapple, peeled, cored
- 2 teaspoons ground cinnamon
- 1/2 cup coconut sugar
- 3 tablespoons melted unsalted butter

Method:

1. Switch on the air fryer, insert fryer basket, grease it with olive oil, then shut with its lid, set the fryer at 400 degrees F, and preheat for 10 minutes.
2. Meanwhile, place sugar in a bowl, add cinnamon, and stir until mixed.
3. Cut pineapple into spears, brush them generously with melted butter, and then coat them with the sugar-cinnamon mixture, pressing lightly.
4. Open the fryer, add pineapple in it in a single layer, close with its lid and cook for 10 minutes until nicely golden and crispy, shaking the basket every 5 minutes and brushing with melted butter halfway through.
5. When air fryer beeps, open its lid, transfer pineapple pieces onto a serving plate, keep them warm and cook remaining pineapple for 8 minutes.
6. Serve straight away.

Nutrition Value:

- Calories: 295 Cal
- Fat: 8 g
- Carbs: 57 g
- Protein: 1 g
- Fiber: 3 g

Key Lime Cupcakes

Preparation time: 20 minutes
Cooking time: 25 minutes
Servings: 6

Ingredients:

- 2 limes, juiced, zested
- 1 teaspoon vanilla extract, unsweetened
- ¼ cup swerve caster sugar
- 8 ounces Greek yogurt
- 2 eggs
- 1 egg yolk
- 7 ounces cream cheese, softened

Method:

1. Place yogurt in a bowl, add cream cheese and mix with a hand mixer until creamy.
2. Then whisk in eggs, egg yolk, lime juice, lime zest, and vanilla until incorporated and then evenly divide the mixture between six silicone muffin cups, reserving the rest of the batter for later use.
3. Switch on the air fryer, insert fryer basket, grease it with olive oil, then shut with its lid, set the fryer at 320 degrees F, and preheat for 5 minutes.
4. Open the fryer, stack muffin cups in it, close with its lid, cook for 10 minutes and then continue cooking for 10 minutes at 350 degrees F until thoroughly cooked.
5. When air fryer beeps, open its lid, transfer muffins to a wire rack, and let cool for 10 minutes.
6. Then place reserved batter in a piping bag, then pipe the batter onto the cupcake and refrigerate them for 4 hours until the top has set.
7. Serve straight away.

Nutrition Value:

- Calories: 218 Cal
- Fat: 14 g
- Carbs: 13 g
- Protein: 9 g
- Fiber: 0 g

Conclusion

This cookbook will let you experience Mexican-style home-cooking with your air fryer. These flavorful dishes are hand-picked to ensure you have a hearty collection of the best recipes on hand at all times. There is no doubt that this cookbook is the ultimate companion book to any Mexican Air Fryer. You are guaranteed to find a wonderful selection of traditional, modern, and alternative Mexican air fryer recipes inside.

Enjoy delicious and fresh Mexican meals in just minutes with these easy recipes using the most versatile appliance in the kitchen—Mexican Air Fryer!

www.ingramcontent.com/pod-product-compliance
Lightning Source LLC
Chambersburg PA
CBHW081402070526
44583CB00020B/2637